LIBRARY CONTESTS

A How-To-Do-It Manual®

Kathleen R. T. Imhoff
Ruthie Maslin

HOW-TO-DO-IT MANUALS

NUMBER 152

NEAL-SCHUMAN PUBLISHERS, INC.
New York,   London

Published by Neal-Schuman Publishers, Inc.
100 William St., Suite 2004
New York, NY 10038

ISBN-13: 978-1-55570-559-6
ISBN-10: 1-55570-559-6

Library of Congress Cataloging-in-Publication Data

Imhoff, Kathleen.
    Library contests : a how-to-do-it manual / Kathleen R. T. Imhoff, Ruthie Maslin.
        p. cm. — (How-to-do-it manuals for librarians ; no. 152)
        Includes bibliographical references and index.
        ISBN 1-55570-559-6 (alk. paper)
    1. Libraries—Public relations. 2. Advertising—Libraries. 3. Libraries and community. 4. Contests. I. Maslin, Ruthie, 1966– II. Title.
Z716. 3I44   2007
021. 7—dc22   2006033177

CONTENTS

LIST OF FIGURES

PREFACE

People love a good contest. A challenge, the chance to win a prize, or simple curiosity makes a smart guessing game or attention-grabbing drawing irresistible. Whether you design a contest to attract patrons, energize the community about a new service, or generate publicity buzz, your event can be a unique treat. *Library Contests: A How-To-Do-It Manual* offers clear, detailed instructions on how to develop and run a new event or improve an existing one. Sponsoring contests can be enjoyable and entertaining once you learn the ropes. Veteran advice mixed with real-world examples and our step-by-step approach will help you avoid common pitfalls. We also offer simple tips for success. Paying attention to each detail may seem like a great deal of work, but the effort is worth it. If you follow the steps in the chapters ahead, your contest should run smoothly.

Library Contests: A How-To-Do-It Manual is designed for staff at all levels. Novices learning to plan, organize, and run contests will find tried-and-true ideas. Seasoned contest planners will be inspired by fresh viewpoints and new perspectives. Upper-level administrators will find practical discussions of the pros and cons of contests, including large-scale benefits such as media attention and increased library use. Workers running an event for which planning is already complete will learn where and how they fit into the larger project.

There are nine steps to a well-planned and well-executed contest. Each of the first nine chapters tackles one of these steps. We recommend reading this guide from first page to last for those in the thinking or early development stages. If you are in the middle of a contest, flip directly to the chapters you need most. If you are unsure about contest development, start with Chapter 10, then read Chapters 1 through 9 in order, since these present an iterative overview of the process.

- Step 1, "Select the Contest Planner and Develop Community Partnerships," covers the process of choosing a planner for your contests and explains the importance of collaborating with other community players. To facilitate brainstorming, this chapter includes a list of partners worth seeking along with a few that should be avoided.

- Step 2, "Establish the Contest Goals and Estimate the Budget," delineates seven possible sources of fiscal support. By carefully balancing your options, you can guarantee that your event achieves maximum success with minimal budgetary impact.

- Step 3, "Define the Contest Type, Audience, and Theme," guides you through the process of determining whom a contest is intended to serve. Whether you ultimately decide to serve a broad spectrum of patrons or a specific group of users, this step is crucial.

- Step 4, "Determine Eligibility Criteria and Rules," identifies five main eligibility factors and guides you through the process of writing rules, creating an entry form, and devising a tip sheet.

- Step 5, "Schedule the Contest," suggests ways to increase a contest's effect by tying it to a season, occasional event, or one-time happening.

- Step 6, "Select the Prize," examines the best strategies for choosing an appropriate reward for winners. A comprehensive list of eleven prize categories with many specific suggestions is included.

- Step 7, "Choose Judges and Set Judging Criteria," outlines the judging process. The process of finding and selecting judges is covered from start to finish. You will learn also how to ensure that the judging is consistent and fair.

- Step 8, "Promote the Contest," will help you rejuvenate your marketing strategy with successful publicity ideas from libraries across the country. Suggestions for promoting your contest are included.

- Step 9, "Evaluate Success," shows you how to determine whether a completed contest achieved its intended effects. By using the tools in this chapter, you can gather the greatest possible amount of detail in evaluations from both audience and staff.

- Step 10, "Now, Put the Plan in Motion: Four Model Contests," presents four sample contests, describing how the planners worked through each of the steps outlined in Chapters 1 through 9. The programs are ranked by difficulty to give you a sense of what to expect when creating your own projects.

No doubt part of your institution's mission is to persuade patrons that the library is a friendly, fun place to learn. Contests are a great way to entice users to pass through the doors. A well-run contest has the potential to reach far beyond its immediate effects.

ACKNOWLEDGMENTS

This book would not have been possible without students in a Syracuse University marketing class discovering that there was no book on library contests. Our reserve of inspiration came from all of the amazing, creative library staffs from around the world who have made contests a vital part of their programming. We thank our families for their support and a special thanks goes to our mews, Bridgett the cat.

INTRODUCTION: WHY HOLD A LIBRARY CONTEST?

The answer begins with another question. What do you want to accomplish with the contest?

- Do you want to involve a particular segment of your community or patron base in a specific library program? This might be a group you have not had great success in engaging in the past, or perhaps it is a group whose participation in your programs has flagged and you are hoping to reengage them. For example, you may have a successful adult reading or film series, but you have discovered that high school student attendance at the programs is nearly nonexistent. Organizing an essay contest about one of the authors or films featured in your series with the grand prize of a college scholarship may stimulate high school attendance.

- Do you want to increase use and circulation of a new collection? Customers might read a certain number of books in the collection to earn prizes like discount coupons, movie tickets, or library logo items. Incentive contests are a fun way to introduce new collections.

- Do you want to achieve larger attendance at a special event? You might, for example, want to have a good showing at the opening of a new branch. Here, a contest in which each person who attends earns a chance at winning the grand prize of an autographed copy of a hot new book, a framed architect's drawing of the new branch, or even something as simple as dinner for two at a local restaurant will bolster your crowd.

- Do you want to get local press coverage of your program or new service? Sometimes it is hard for libraries to get the attention of the local newspapers or TV stations. A contest may be different enough to get a news editor to take note of the event and send out a reporter.

Contests are often closely connected to other programming taking place at the library. For example, most reading programs for adults or children have a contest component built into them. Participants are trying to complete the required number of books or achieve the required amount of time spent reading in order to win prizes or incentive items. It is clear that holding a contest can help you and your library accomplish a specific purpose—for instance, raising your summer reading program participation by 10 percent—but keeping your eye on the broad-based benefits is just as important.

BENEFITS OF A CONTEST

Contests generally yield at least three important benefits:

- Door traffic will increase. Any contest you promote even minimally will draw in additional people, whether it is to pick up or deliver an entry form, to check on progress, or just to view the winning results. All these individuals are potential patrons or customers.
- Partnerships will strengthen. This applies to in-house and community partnerships. Your staff will have to collaborate with each other, and because few libraries have all the resources they need at their fingertips, drawing on outside resources will help create external collaborations.
- Community interest and involvement will build. You will increase community interest in your library, your program, or your new service. Unless you hold the contest in the cleaning closet and keep the door closed throughout, *someone* is going to see information about the contest and talk about it to someone else. The next person, in turn, may have an interest or know someone who does.

The broad, long-lasting impacts to be gained from contests are not readily apparent, but they are real. These are also good points to highlight when you are trying to sell the idea to your board of trustees, co-workers, PTA, community partners, and sponsors.

KEY CONSIDERATIONS

The clearer you are about the value of your project, the easier it will be to make the case for it to others. Think through all of the possible details and be ready to field any question that might come your way. The "Determining Factor" questionnaire at the end of this section (see Figure I-1) serves as a checklist for you as you make your decision. Let us look at a few factors in more depth.

- Is a contest consistent with the library's goals and marketing plan? Whether the library's communication and marketing plan is a single page of guidelines or a twenty-page document, you should review the existing plan. Does the contest help the library to meet its goals? It is always easier to create a successful program when it helps everyone achieve their short- and long-term goals. Talk with the library staff to determine if a contest is the best way to help them satisfy their departmental aspirations. Discuss ways in which a contest can work for everyone. An essay contest may help the marketing department promote a system-wide event by encouraging a broad base of participation. That same contest may also help the outreach department meet its goal of getting children more interested in writing. A program that does double duty makes good economic sense.

- Does your library have the staff and budget to offer a contest? This book provides guidelines to help you determine the costs of a contest in money and in staff time. These tools give you some guidance, but you must make the ultimate decision based on the particulars of your situation. Do you have the dollars and the staff time to do the job well?

- Are contests a good fit for your community, school, or campus? Review contests held by other agencies or groups in the area and talk to the planners about their success or lack of success. Learn from their local experience. Keep in mind that some people view contests as a form of gambling even if some skill or talent is required in order to win. In many areas of the United States, the question of whether or not to allow legalized gambling is a controversial issue. If your area of the country is still fighting about legalizing gambling, people there might not be comfortable with certain types of competition as a public relations tool. The same could be true for the staff that you need to have involved in promoting and holding the contest.

KEY QUESTION	YES	NO	NOTES
Does a contest fit into your library's general annual goals?			
Do the contest goals mesh with other library/department goals?			
Do you have enough money and staff time to run a successful contest?			
Do your staff and the library administration support the use of contests in general and this contest in particular?			
Has your library held contests in the past?			
Have those contests been successful?			
Are there other groups in your community having success with contests?			
Have you checked the contest date for possible conflicts with other events in the community and/or library?			
Have you checked this time for possible community tie-ins?			
How long will the contest run?			
Is the contest period long enough to generate the desired number of entries?			
Is this long enough to allow entrants to complete their entries?			

Fill out this questionnaire as objectively as you can. Be sure to fill in the NOTES column, even if your notes are sketchy. These will help you move toward building a plan for the contest. If you answer "No" to three or more of these questions, you should probably rethink the viability of holding a contest in your library or at least hold off planning the contest until some of the "No" issues have been resolved.

Figure I-1. Library Contest Determining Factor Questionnaire

The preparation and planning for a contest can be a lot of work. You may discover halfway through that things are not turning out quite the way you envisioned them. You may even begin to doubt yourself and your ability to achieve your goal, but do not give up. With declining budgets and increasing competition for the public dollar, library contests are an excellent value, generating publicity and community goodwill, helping raise money and awareness of library programs and features, and drawing more patrons and customers through the doors. So, let the contests begin!

1

SELECT THE CONTEST PLANNER AND DEVELOP COMMUNITY PARTNERSHIPS

SELECTING A CONTEST PLANNER

Getting started can be challenging. Someone on the staff comes up with an attractive, fun-sounding library contest. The idea gets shared with others who also think the contest would be a worthwhile effort. Then the idea drifts off and dies. What was missing?

What was missing was the contest planner or planning team, those whose duties are to see the contest through from the idea to a plan, to implementation, and then to evaluation. All successful contests have a designated contest planner or a contest-planning team. They serve as a focal point for the project.

The first decision you need to make to get your contest started is whether a single contest planner or a contest-planning team works best.

CONSIDERING AN INDIVIDUAL PLANNER

A single contest planner is a good route to take if your contest is fairly limited in scope. Contests that involve a single department, grade, classroom in a school, or even library location might be better served by a single contest planner. The type of contest also might dictate a single planner. A "Guess the Number of . . ." contest is fairly easy and straightforward to put together and would not require an entire team to organize. Many essay or writing contests do not need a planning team per se, although you would probably need a team effort to carry out the contest. Finally, the complexity of the contest and the entry requirements, the period of time over which the contest will take place, and the number of partners involved are all factors that must be considered when deciding between a single planner and a team.

For many contests, the children's librarian or a staff member of the children's department is the logical contest planner. Summer reading contests, art contests, and easy guessing contests are often focused on children, so it makes sense to have the contest planner be the person who will be most involved and in whose department most of the contest activities will happen. The children's staff know most of the children who would be eligible to participate in the contest and would be the people most likely to talk up the contest to the young library users.

TIP: Library contests in schools are a good way to get parents involved.

In a school library, the contest planner most frequently is the school media specialist for the same reasons mentioned previously. However, in a school library, the contest planner might also be a volunteer parent. Depending on the level of volunteerism in the school and the work load of the media specialist, a parent volunteer might in fact be the most logical choice for the contest planner. The volunteer might have time to enlist the time and talents of other volunteers as well. The selection of the school library contest planner depends entirely on the local situation, local staff, and level of volunteerism in the school.

In larger public and academic libraries, the contest planner could be the department head or a staff member from the department that is most closely connected to the contest. If the contest is a literary essay contest, the contest planner most likely would be someone from the humanities or literature departments. A photography contest would be headed by someone from the art department. Try to match the contest planner with a person with a background or interest in the topic of the contest. The selected contest planner can bring his or her subject expertise to the contest. Another advantage of selecting a subject expert for the contest planner is the high likelihood that the subject expert personally would know excellent, qualified people who could judge the contest.

In a medium-sized to large library, the person responsible for programming or the person responsible for marketing may be assigned the task of planning for any library contest as part of his or her job responsibilities. This approach creates greater continuity and builds an expertise in the area. If this is the approach used in your library, try to keep the subject expert involved as a resource person.

If you are a one- to three-person library, the library director usually is the person who runs the contest. Another likely scenario in a small library is that the person who comes up with the idea for the contest is the one chosen to be the contest planner. In these cases, it is best to take time to consider if selecting a person to implement the contest just because he or she came up with the idea is the best approach. People who generate ideas are not always the best organizers, planners, or implementers. In a small library situation, consider a community volunteer to be the contest planner.

TIP: Selecting the right planner is key to a successful contest.

Most contests have a single individual as the contest planner. The checklist on page 3 has a column for "person responsible" for task (see Figure 1-1). Depending on the size of the library, this may be the same name all the way through the list. In large libraries, the job tasks may be divided up.

ORGANIZING A PLANNING TEAM

The team approach is often optimal when dealing with a complex contest, like a book-collecting contest in a university. A planning team allows for many voices to be a part of the decision-making process, which makes a contest more well rounded. The size of the library system can determine whether or

Action Item	Date Needed	Person Responsible	Date Completed
Form committee to choose theme & set criteria for entry	May 1	John H. and Fred L.	May 2
Meet with Metro Bank to discuss prize sponsorship	May 7	Larry N.	May 7
Ask Mayor Smith to be Honorary Judge	May 22	John H.	May 15
Meet with marketing dept. to discuss promotions	June 6	Mary E.	June 8
Set-up for announcement party	June 29	Fred L. and committee	
Contest run	June 30– July 31		
Contest announcement party	June 30	Mary E.	
Plan award party	July 20	Mary E.	
Copy entries for committee	August 1	Mike G.	
Initial screening of entries	August 2	Committee	
Deliver short-listed entries to mayor for final judging	August 4	Fred L.	
Invite finalists to award party	August 10	Mary E.	
Announce winner at award party	August 20	Fred L. and Mayor Smith	
Hold evaluation meeting to assess successes and failures of project	August 25	Fred L. and committee	

Figure 1-1. Sample Planning Document for an Essay Contest

not a contest-planning team is set up or not. If a library has branches, it might be helpful to have someone from every branch or region included on a team to increase staff buy-in as well as knowledge and enthusiasm about the contest.

Because there are many skills required to hold a successful contest—organization, attention to detail, engaging others, collaboration, and networking—often the contest-planning team is the best approach to help guarantee a contest that accomplishes its goals. In medium-sized to large-libraries, a team could be composed of many members of the same department or members from several different departments. A summer reading contest might be run by the children's librarians or other children's staff. A logo contest could be run by the marketing department with a representative from each library coordinating the local work. There may be as many ways to set up a contest team as there are libraries.

It even may make more sense to use the efforts and expertise of an existing standing committee within your library rather than convening a new one just for the contest. A staff activities committee, programming committee, or publicity committee that already exists might be assigned the responsibility for the contest. The choice of the appropriate committee will vary by the type and size of the library sponsoring the contest. If an existing committee takes on the role of the contest-planning team, make sure the committee members and the chair are clear ahead of time about their responsibilities and authority with respect to the contest, as these may differ slightly from the committee's original charge and purpose. Clarifying the committee's expanded charge and authority will simplify the committee's work and help members be more effective.

CHOOSING CONTEST LEADERS

Each library should evaluate if a single person, an existing committee, or an existing department should have the contest-planning responsibility or if a separate contest committee needs to be established. Any of the methods can work. Each has its own advantages or disadvantages. Consider how the library has assigned responsibilities in the past and evaluate past successes. Talk to other departments or previous staff and volunteers about other library contests. After thinking about all of the options outlined above, select the one that has the best chance of success for your library.

The people involved determine the project's success. In selecting both the planner and team members, enthusiasm and willingness are two of the most important ingredients. If the person selected as the contest planner already feels overworked, has no interest in the contest, or thinks it is not in the library's mission to hold contests, it is probably in the project's best interest to select someone else for the job. That clearly is not the background of a creative contest planner. If the contest is complex, the person selected as either planner or team member must be allocated the time to do the contest-related work without negative impact on the rest of his or her work. If possible, ask for staff volunteers for these jobs, rather than assign them. A willing, enthusiastic volunteering staff member has a greater chance of success than an assigned, overworked contest subject expert. Sometimes, people volunteer for what they consider a fun project, for example, running a contest, to get out of doing their regular work. The most competent contest planner or team member is one who is capable, hard working, able to meet deadlines, able to organize others, enthusiastic, and willing to take on the assignment and enjoy it. Figure 1-1, Sample Planning Document for an Essay Contest, lists the tasks required of the person or people who run the contest. It would be helpful to review the list and see if the potential contest planners or team members have these skills. Collaboration, attention to detail, and ability to see a project through to completion in a timely fashion are integral competencies for a contest planner or contest team member.

Once you have decided who will run your contest, it is important before you go forward to look to see if you should or could improve the contest through partnering with others in the community. There are several other times in the contest-planning process that you will consider possible partnerships, but it is important to think about partners right from the start.

FORMING COMMUNITY PARTNERSHIPS

As their name implies, contest partners can be thought of as co-planners and co-workers in producing a successful library contest. Since many libraries are already seeking to engage partners in many aspects of their work, extending that idea of partnership to contest planning and execution is a natural next step. Partnerships can offer many benefits to the library and to the partners. Good partnerships may help increase exposure and publicity, spread the workload, share the cost, maximize resources and minimize liabilities, bring in new ideas that lead to innovation, and increase community support. These advantages should be mutually beneficial. One-sided partnerships can actually be worse for the project than having no partners at all.

TIP: Library contests provide an excellent opportunity to form and cement partnerships.

When seeking partners in your community, on your campus, or even within your own organization, it is important to stress the mutual benefits and responsibilities of the relationship. Being clear from the start can save a lot of frustration down the line. Do not be afraid to outline your expectations when approaching a potential partner. Do not be timid about asking for what you need to put on your ideal contest or program. Do not skimp on the details of what the partners can expect from their participation. Remember, good partnerships can be a win-win situation for all involved, and when they work well, they begin to build the foundation for long-term relationships. A partner who has a positive experience will be much more likely to support future library endeavors.

While many of the benefits of partnerships discussed here do not involve actual money, they do offer measurable value, and we are all interested in adding value to our undertakings. When approaching potential partners, be prepared to tell them succinctly the value of the partnership to them and to the library and the community. Be real—do not exaggerate or oversell the value.

One of the biggest values of a partnership is the exposure or publicity connected with it. Even without a big marketing budget or heavy marketing efforts, the involvement of partners in a project naturally increases the publicity and exposure value of the project. The more people who are involved, the more people will know about what is going on. Do not underestimate the power of word-of-mouth advertising. Each player in the contest brings his or her own circle of friends, family, neighbors, and co-workers to the table. When you add in the concerted marketing efforts partners can bring into the mix, the value increases exponentially. In many cases, a corporate partner will have a dedicated marketing department and budget to bring to the project. Partnering with the library can improve the company's image as a good neighbor and good corporate citizen.

TIP: Use contest partners to expand your reach.

Sometimes the situation is reversed. Your library may have its own marketing department with promotion of the contest already built into its budget, but your business or community partner does not. The business or community partner, on the other hand, may be able to provide prizes or people-power your library cannot afford. Spreading the workload is an added value from partnering on a library contest. The old adage holds true here: Many hands make light work. Putting together even a small contest can be a lot of work for one person, but if one person takes care of prizes, one person produces the entry forms and publicity flyers, and one person processes the entries, the job becomes manageable for everyone.

Sharing the cost is always a benefit. Depending on the financial situation of your own library, you may or may not want to move this benefit to the top of your list. Keep in mind that partnerships may not include an exchange of actual money. After figuring out the costs of your contest, you might start by deciding which costs your library definitely can cover and which will be a stretch. Then consider possible partners who might be able to cover those costs.

PICKING PERFECT PARTNERS

TIP: Use a library contest as a means of getting a foot in the door with a local company. This can lead to expanded future partnerships on other library initiatives.

Like ice cream, partnerships come in all different flavors. They can vary by role, extent of involvement, length of time, and many other factors. Partners can actually work side by side with you on doing the work of the contest. Sponsorship is a type of partnership that involves more cost sharing than work sharing. You may even have different sponsors for different parts of the contest. For example, a local printing company can sponsor production of your posters and entry forms, while a local catering company might sponsor the awards ceremony reception. Sponsors may also offer a prize. It may be something—a good or service—that their company produces. Sponsors may also bring to the table things necessary to the contest but ones you may not automatically think of, like exhibit space for the entries in a poster contest or use of their auditorium for the awards presentation.

A photography contest may be presented in partnership with a famous local photographer or photography studio. An essay contest might be sponsored by your city's newspaper. Finally, the library might form partnerships for a contest that can be part of an effort to promote a community effort together. Perhaps your community has identified adult literacy as a priority for the coming year. The library might partner with a local bookstore to offer an essay contest for adult new learners that includes writing classes before the contest starts. The grand prize might be a small personal library of thirty books or a subscription to the local newspaper or magazines of interest.

As you consider potential partners for your contest, start to think creatively about whom you would like to see at the table. Good partnership experiences on small projects can lead to longer and larger partnership commitments for library projects. Consider the long-term implications of your partnership choices beyond the scope of a single contest. Whom would you like to see more involved in your library in general? That person or business or organization might make a good contest partner. Partnerships on contests are also a good way to test a potential longer-term relationship. Because they tend to be relatively narrow in scope, contests can be viewed as a microcosm of larger partner relationships. By involving a potential partner from the start, you can see how you work together on goal-setting, planning, publicity, execution, and evaluation.

Consider partnerships with other libraries, with other departments within your library system or organization, or with volunteer groups affiliated with your library or organization. For example, public libraries can partner with entire schools or even school systems. School libraries can partner with other schools or even with classes or teachers within the school. On a university or college campus, a music library may partner with a law library or even one of the departments on campus.

> **TIP:** Partner with other libraries in your area to establish a network of colleagues and resources.

A key contest partner for many libraries large and small is the Friends of the Library organization. Partnering with your library's Friends group on a contest is a great way to strengthen the relationship with these valuable library volunteers. It gives both groups a well-focused project with success built into it from the start. It provides great publicity opportunities. The Friends as a sponsor can bring much-needed volunteer time and/or money into the project.

Consider the following list of possibilities to help you think of possible partners in your own community:

- Library-related partners such as bookstores, publishers, book distributors, or local authors
- Banks
- Airlines
- Local pro sports franchises like professional ball clubs or hockey teams
- Local media, like TV and radio stations, magazines, e-zines, blogs, and newspapers
- Restaurants
- Nonprofit organizations, like the local arts council or adult literacy center

- Theaters
- Department and discount stores
- Local or regional foundations or philanthropic organizations
- Community groups like the Junior League and local AARP chapters
- Local or state government
- Historic preservation groups or organizations
- Celebrities or high-profile people from the community
- Tourism boards
- Chambers of commerce
- Civic groups like the Lions Club, Kiwanis, or Rotary Club
- Professional organizations like a society of civil engineers or the board of realtors
- Hospitals and doctors' offices
- Churches
- Law firms
- Public relations firms
- Pet stores and veterinarians
- Local industries like car and computer manufacturers
- Local offices of national companies, like United Parcel Service (UPS), Amazon.com, and Fruit of the Loom
- Franchises of national chains
- Your state library or special libraries in your region

TIP: In your early contest planning, take time to brainstorm potential partners.

Determine the community connections your staff has, such as family business ties, community organization involvement, faith community involvement, school connections, and volunteer connections. For instance, you may have a staff member whose husband teaches art at a local college or university. Right away you have a good source for a judging partnership with the art department. Make a list of the businesses that are near your library. The grocery store next door to the library may be willing to donate refreshments and help you plan your awards ceremony. Once you decide the theme of your contest, check the phone book or city directory for businesses or organizations listed in categories related to your contest. These are all potential partners.

The Anchorage (AK) Municipal Libraries had more than twenty businesses and organizations involved in one of their recent summer reading programs, as shown in Figure 1-2. Bringing partners on board is an excellent way to stimulate broad-based community support for your library. Being a partner with the library is good exposure for businesses in the area. It is a winning combination.

**Figure 1-2. Anchorage Municipal Libraries Summer
Reading Program Sponsors
(Printed with permission of Anchorage Municipal Libraries.)**

Some examples of partnership possibilities for specific types and themes of contests are listed below. You can come up with similar possible partners using resources in your own community.

1. Essay or poetry contest—local school, college, or university English departments, community writing groups, newspapers, book publishers, authors in the area
2. Arbor Day poster contest—local chapters of the Sierra Club or other area conservation groups, nurseries and garden shops, national or state forests in the area, local orchards, an arboretum, university agricultural department, local 4-H extension office
3. Photography contest—local camera shops, framing shops, photo developing centers, camera clubs, local newspapers, high school or college art departments, public relations or advertising firms, well-known local photographers
4. "Beat the Heat" summer reading contest—air conditioning sales or repair businesses, local fan stores or home improvement stores, pool supply and installation companies, ice cream producers or retailers, ice companies, local water theme parks, city parks and recreation departments, YMCAs, YWCAs, local ice skating rinks

IDENTIFYING UNSUITABLE PARTNERSHIPS

Not all partners are good for your library and its image in the community. Think of potential contest partners as potential employees. Check them out. Examine their past community involvement. Find out their mission statement. Carefully consider the types of potential partners discussed below.

Avoiding Dubious Affiliates

This has to be determined by the standards of your own community, and the criteria certainly may change over time. For example, if you live in a dry town (one in which liquor sales are prohibited), you will probably want to avoid partnering with a distillery or brewery from the next town or county.

An example of how a partnership can go awry is the public library that recruited a famous professional athlete to award the prize to the winner of its contest for children. Soon after the involvement of this athlete had been announced, he made headlines for getting into a huge fight and beating up several other players. He had turned from a positive role model to a negative one overnight, and he had to be abandoned as a program partner.

Tobacco stores and producers may be considered a part of this category, especially if the contest is aimed at children. In recent years, many big tobacco companies have made an attempt to create programs and partnerships that positively impact youth in response to the negative publicity and settlements from numerous lawsuits. You will have to determine if this partnership is a viable option for your own community. If you live in a tobacco-producing state in a community that derives a big part of its livelihood from tobacco production and sales, you and your community may view this issue differently than people who live elsewhere.

Businesses that may have questioned or questionable business practices should be avoided as contest partners. This category might include a business where the CEO is under indictment or a company that is publicly considering bankruptcy. Companies that may have violated EPA regulations or have sexual harassment or racial discrimination charges against them also should be avoided. When considering business partners, it is always wise to put your reference staff to work to check them out before you commit to working with them.

> **TIP:** Choose your partners carefully.

Steering Clear of Politics

If there is an important election coming up in your community, you may see an increase in offers for candidates to participate in your programs. This is dangerous ground to tread because you run the risk of appearing to support one candidate or issue over the others. This can get tricky, for instance, when the incumbent mayor who is running for re-election offers to be a judge for your National Library Week essay contest. The mayor is often a good selection for these types of situations because such a selection builds goodwill between the library and city government and has a built-in publicity value. However, in an election year particularly, this would not be a politically neutral choice to make and thus should be avoided.

Depending on your community, you also may want to avoid partnering with religious or faith-based organizations. Individuals, organizations, or businesses that support or are publicly identified with one side of a hot issue in your community also should be avoided.

In any potentially controversial situation, you and your contest team must make the determination of whether or not the partnership is worth the cost in terms of the library's image and reputation in the community. Increased competition for public dollars may make offers from questionable partners more appealing. However, you need to consider the pros and cons of such alliances carefully.

CHAPTER SUMMARY

Getting started on a library contest can be the hardest part. Once you have determined who will be involved in the contest, from planning to partners, you have made a solid start. With a well-organized contest planner, team, or committee and strong, involved partners, your contest already has moved closer to a positive conclusion.

2 ESTABLISH THE CONTEST GOALS AND ESTIMATE THE BUDGET

ESTABLISHING GOALS

Establishing the goals for your library contest may be the most significant step in making it the success you want it to be. As the contest planner, the task of guiding goal setting and clearly communicating those goals to everyone involved in the project is an important part of your job. The Introduction outlined briefly some reasons a library might decide to hold a contest and some of the general benefits of doing so. These ideas included promoting use of a new service or particular collection, increasing involvement in library programs among your target audience, involving partners, and heightening general awareness of the library in the community or on campus. Brainstorming along these lines with your planning team or other library or school staff is a good start to formalizing the goals for the contest.

The contest planner or planning team can approach the task of goal setting in different ways, depending on the scope of the contest, breadth of partner and community involvement, and the financial and personnel resources available to commit to the project. Keep in mind that contests should be fun. They are a way to get people involved in the library in an entertaining way.

GOALS VERSUS OBJECTIVES

Before you get started with this part of the contest plan, take a moment to note how the terms *goals* and *objectives* are used in this book. Depending on the type or size of your library, the management style used, your library's past planning approaches, and even accepted local usage, the definitions of these terms vary widely. A goal is often used to describe the overall reason you are doing something, while an objective is seen as an action step that can be measured. In this book the terms are used fairly interchangeably. Just be aware that the way you and your planning team use them should correspond to the way others in your library and in other community organizations do.

GENERAL GOALS

One approach is to consider general benefits as discussed in the Introduction. Many contests strive to build public awareness and recognition. Others aim for the production of something useful to a wide number of people, like those selecting the best book in the state or creating a public work of art or a permanent addition to a library collection. These objectives will vary according to the library holding the contest. For example, a school media specialist may want to get high school students more excited about using the library, while an academic librarian may want to increase student and public awareness of a particular field of scholarly research or a special university program or resource.

If the planning team decides to go this route, a key general goal to consider is library growth, whether that is tallied by circulation increases, addition of library card holders, expansion of funding, expansion of services, or a rise in door or Web site traffic. By their very nature, contests attract more people to the library, and thus they have a very direct tie to library growth. A clever contest that stimulated more traffic was the Follow the Nickel Trail contest put on by the David A. Howe Library in Wellsville, New York. As part of the culmination of the library's Read Your Way West Adult Summer Reading Program, library staff placed nickels in books about the West. If the person checking out the book found a nickel in the book, that person was automatically entered in the drawing for a U.S. Mint Westward Expansion nickel proof set. A brochure for this program is shown in Figure 2-1.

GROWTH OF PARTICULAR CUSTOMER SEGMENTS

Contests can also encourage the growth of particular customer segments. Contests for children are particularly successful in this category, because the children typically do not come to the library by themselves. They usually have someone with them, so essentially you are building patronage two for the price of one. A colorful, contemporary, exciting contest can be very effective in drawing teens into the library. The Kalamazoo Public Library in Michigan holds an annual teen summer reading game that is always a big hit. Teens can win prizes and earn raffle tickets for big prize drawings by reading "anything with pages" (see Figures 2-2 and 2-3). Additional raffle tickets can be earned by reading something from a particular genre or attending events at the library. More library usage strengthens the case for more library funding and resources, and a positive growth cycle ensues.

The King County Library System in Washington created a unique teen contest. They awarded "book bucks" for every page a teen read during the summer. The goal of the contest was to keep teens reading during the summer.

WEEKLY PRIZE DRAWINGS FROM AREA MERCHANTS

L'Italia Restaurant
Tami's Floral Expressions
Beef Haus Restaurant
Hamilton Shoes
Music Alley
Hart's Meats

HOW IT WORKS

1. Read any books of your choice. Submit an entry form for each book. Place entry forms in box located at the reading program display near main desk at the library.
2. Library staff will draw a winner each Monday. Staff will call winners and post their names. To qualify, you must have a current library card. The library staff will gladly update your card or issue a new card. Library cards are free.
3. Prizes must be picked up by September 5, 2005.

LOOK FORWARD TO THESE SPECIAL DRAWINGS AT THE END OF THE PROGRAM

Follow the Nickel Trail

We've placed nickels in books about the West. If we find a nickel when you check it out, we'll enter you in a drawing for a U.S. Mint 2005 Westward Expansion nickel proof set!

Conquer the Great Falls

At the end of the program, the patron who's read and submitted the most entries for weekly drawings during the summer will win a George Foreman grill!

EXPLORE THE UNKNOWN... **READ!**

The David A. Howe Public Library
155 N. Main St.
Wellsville, NY 14895
585 593-3410

www.davidahowelibrary.org

READ YOUR WAY WEST
ADULT SUMMER READING PROGRAM

PRESENTED BY THE DAVID A. HOWE LIBRARY

June 27—August 8

COMMEMORATING THE 200TH ANNIVERSARY OF THE LEWIS & CLARK EXPEDITION 1804—1806

Figure 2-1. Read Your Way West
(Reproduced by permission of The David A. Howe Public Library, Mary Jacobs, past director.)

The Friends of the Federal Way Libraries sponsored the event through donations to purchase big-ticket electronic items and refreshments for the auction party. Local businesses donated other prizes. Over a seven-week period, teens in this contest read 1,932 books for a total of 521,364 pages. After the end of the program, the library held an auction in which teens with book bucks were able to bid on prizes. The teens who participated in the contest and attended the auction event received a nine-page brochure with pictures and descriptions of the seventy-nine prizes available. Prizes included MP3 players, CD players, a Nintendo DS Lite, a flash drive, gift certificates, and books (see Figure 2-4). Those who did not win a bid on a prize were given a bag of chocolate.

TIP: Make the contest work for you and the library, not vice versa.

Figure 2-2. Kalamazoo Remix Contest Front Page (Reproduced by permission of the Kalamazoo Public Library. Kevin King, teen librarian; Laura Hoppe, graphic design; Paul Sizer, logo art.)

Figure 2-3. Kalamazoo Remix Contest Inside Game
(Reproduced with permission of the Kalamazoo Public Library. Kevin King, teen librarian; Laura Hoppe, graphic design; Paul Sizer, logo art.)

USING ESTABLISHED GOALS

Another goal-setting approach is to consider established goals for the library or a particular department, branch, or school within the system. These may be current fiscal-year goals or broader goals that are part of the library's long-range plan. Coordinating the goals of a specific program with those of the larger system makes sense.

Regardless of the approach your team uses, taking time to brainstorm ideas at the start is helpful. Brainstorming can be as simple as sitting down

Figure 2-4. Michele McLaughlin, Teen Services Librarian, King County Library System, Auctions Off a Book Bucks Prize (see Figure 2-4a).
(Used by permission. Michele McLaughlin, Teen Services Librarian, King County Library System, with thanks to Dawn Rutherford, Teen Services Librarian, King County Library System.)

over lunch with a group of interested people and discussing how a contest could fit into the library's plan. Or it could be a several-hour session convening all partners and planners. It is not really the number of people involved but the quality of the ideas generated that will help you complete this part of the plan.

2007 TEEN SUMMER READING PROGRAM
JUNE 1–AUGUST 1

BOOK BUCKS AUCTION

If you are in middle/junior or high school, bring your **Read Three Get One Free** forms, lled out with three thoughtful and unique reviews, into **Federal Way Regional Library or Federal Way 320th Library.** Every page you read (every 2 pages for Graphic Novels/Manga) will count as a $1 Book Buck. A 200 page book=$200 Book Bucks to bid on great stu ($100 Book Bucks if itís a graphic novel). Listening to books on cassette/CD also counts! Then spend your Book Bucks at the auction at the Federal Way Regional Library on August 11 at 1pm! Pizza will be served!

Read 3 Get 1 Free forms are available in the library or at **www.kcls.org/read3.**

**Possible prizes include MP3 players, CD Players and/or a Nintendo DS LiteÆ
plus electronic games, gift certi cates & more!**
(You must come to the auction to redeem your Book Bucks)

FEDERAL WAY REGIONAL LIBRARY
FEDERAL WAY 320TH LIBRARY
253.838.3668

**Generous support for this program provided by the KCLS
Foundation and the Friends of the Federal Way Libraries.**

these districts assume no responsibility for the conduct or safety during the event/activity/o er. In consideration for the privilege to distribute these materials, the Auburn, Federal Way, Highline and Shoreline School Districts shall be held harmless from any cause of action, claim or petition led in any court or administrative tribunal arising out of the distribution of these materials, including all costs, attorneyís fees and judgments or awards.

**Figure 2-4a. Teens participating in the 2007 Teen Summer Reading Program of the Federal Way Regional Library and Federal Way 320th Library of the King County Library System in Washington earn "Book Bucks" for reading. They can use the Book Bucks to bid on prizes at the end of the program.
(Used by permission. King County Library System.)**

COMMITTING GOALS TO PAPER

Formalizing your ideas and the results of your team's brainstorming sessions in clearly stated goals is the next logical step, bringing together elements of the purpose and objective of your contest. These goals should be easy to articulate to all involved, and they should be measurable in some way to help facilitate more useful evaluation at the end of the project.

You can use this list of general goals to help you define goals specific to your library and your situation.

Potential goals might include:

- Increase target audience participation. When a library is failing to get members of a particular demographic through the door, a contest targeted to that group can be a useful tool for drawing them in.

- Advertise a particular service. You can test your success with this type of goal by building in an evaluative tool that will help measure how many people know about the service when the contest is done. A quick one-day poll of everyone who walks through the door would work. Or you could even hold a secondary contest through your Web site by having a quick poll and entering the name of everyone who responds into a drawing for a special prize.

- Highlight or introduce a new service. Contests can be a fantastic way to inform the public about new downloadable books, important local history acquisitions, or other significant changes in service.

- Involve partners. and use It is important that a library not only serve its community but also belong to it, and contests can be a helpful step toward realizing this ideal.

- Heighten awareness and use of the library overall. You easily measure your achievement of this goal by examining circulation during the contest period or through a patron count.

- Motivate staff to be invested in the library's overall mission. It is not just the public that gets excited about contests; staff often does as well. Not only do these events introduce an exciting element into the work week, they also allow for fun and different interactions with patrons.

- Energize patrons. Even today, some library users still think of the library as a dull, quiet space, out of touch with the dynamism of the real world. A cool contest can show them that libraries are engaging and full of vitality.

Once you have clarified and formalized your contest goals, write them down and pass them out to everyone involved. Ask for feedback, and make changes where the team thinks it is appropriate. Having the written goal statements as a reference point helps everyone stay focused throughout the duration of the project. Goal statements should be fairly short and very specific. Often they will have quantifiable components, stating specific target audience numbers, percent of circulation increase, or number of new library cards issued. Mixing qualitative and quantitative goal statements up front makes evaluation at the end of the contest much easier. Qualitative goals address the philosophical underpinnings of the contest—what changes in perception, attitudes, or behaviors you hope to achieve. Quantitative goals, on the other hand, are quite literally those whose results you can count or measure. The mix can also help ensure that there will be some element of success in the undertaking regardless of the overall results. For instance, a goal of heightening awareness of a new Web site service like downloadable audio books as a qualitative statement opens the door to success whether forty people tried the new service or 4,000 did. Finally, make sure each statement focuses on a single goal. Some examples of goal statements include the following:

> **TIP:** Careful planning and preparation can make everyone involved in your library contest a true WINNER!

Qualitative goal statements:

- Use an art display of winners for the lobby of the new branch library to show the public that libraries are more than books.
- Design a logo for the bookmobile that showcases its history.
- Involve middle-school-age boys in summer reading activities in the branches.

Quantitative goal statements:

- Improve the summer reading completion rate by 5 percent.
- Attract an audience of at least sixty people from the community to the opening of the new central library computer lab.
- Increase room count of the local history collection by 10 percent.
- Raise the number of unique Web site hits by 20,000.

Clear goals help measure success. They act as a unifying force in the completion of the project. They can keep the planning team as well as the library staff focused. Do not be afraid to aim high. At the same time, keep your goals manageable by viewing the contest as a part of the library's overall plan for the year.

After establishing goals, you should do a preliminary estimate of the cost involved in terms of dollars, staff time, and in-kind services. This will help you map out a budget for the contest. The next part of this chapter goes into detail on sources of funding for the contest and guides you in the development of a budget.

CREATING THE BUDGET

Although there is no one universal cost formula to guide the contest planner in determining the costs that could be incurred in a contest, costs need to be planned to test the feasibility of holding a contest. A checklist of items that affect the contest budget and need to be considered includes the following:

1. The cost of the prizes or recognition items
2. The cost of promotion, including

    a. promotional items such as notices, bookmarks, flyers, signs
    b. judging costs, including scoring sheets and travel and food expenses for judges
    c. printing
    d. advertising

3. The cost of the recognition event
4. The cost of staff time
5. The length of the contest

Estimating specific costs for particular budget items varies widely by locale. Costs for catering and printing will probably be higher in large cities, for example. Bigger libraries might draw larger crowds, translating into a higher cost for a recognition event than what could be expected in a smaller library. In general, however, the contest planner or planning team should find it fairly easy to assign cost estimates to a particular item to create a fairly realistic budget.

Determining the cost of staff time might seem a bit tricky. The contest is part of the library's programming, and that means it is a part of staff's regular work time, right? If holding a Guess the Number of Jellybeans in the Jar on the Information Desk contest involves fifteen hours each from three different employees, it might be financially prudent to consider the value of the contest in terms of its cost. For the first contest you hold, it is probably easiest to estimate how much staff time the planner or planning team wants to commit to the project. For example, if a school media specialist is holding a poster contest for fifth graders and the contest is expected to run three weeks, he or she might decide to spend three hours a week on the contest plus three hours for planning and five hours for judging and the awards ceremony. The media specialist could then estimate the cost of his or her time in relationship to the contest by multiplying the hourly salary by the seventeen hours he or she anticipates committing to the contest.

If the department, library, or school media center envisions making contests a regular, budgeted part of the annual programming plan, then a more formalized approach may be needed. The most straightforward approach to separating the time spent on a specific project from general work time is to do a detailed time study for a set period of time—two weeks, for instance. This approach can be modified easily to work with a contest. First, designate a start time for the work study. Ideally, this would begin when planning begins. Then create a chart with each workday divided into half-hour or even fifteen-minute blocks. Each staff member involved makes brief notations indicating what he or she does during each block of time. If the planner or planning team is only using the time study to determine contest costs, then staff only need to note time spent on the contest on the time study sheets. The time study should run the entire length of the contest. Once the study is completed, a simple analysis will reveal how much time is spent on each aspect of the contest.

Remember when developing the estimated budget for the contest that closely connected with the cost to the library is adequacy of the award to the contest participant. The contest planner might be satisfied with the low cost of the contest, but investigation could show that the contest winner would win so small a prize that there would be little incentive for a person to enter the contest. If this is the case, the contest planner should increase the value of the prizes or the contest should be dropped.

Determining the cost of prizes is fairly straightforward, as is estimating printing costs. More difficult to plan for is the cost of announcement receptions because it is next to impossible to know how many people will be attending unless you enforce a strict RSVP process, which few librarians and library staff have time to do. Ask others in the library who have hosted receptions in the past what the general cost was and derive your estimate from those figures.

SEVEN SOURCES OF CONTEST FUNDING

Once you have outlined a basic budget, you need to figure out how you are going to pay for it. There are seven major sources of funding for library contests:

1. The library's budget
2. The Friends of the Library
3. A library foundation

4. Donations
5. In-kind services
6. Sponsorships
7. Combination of the above methods

The next section explores ways to pay for the contest. The more advance planning there is for the contest, the better chance to form partnerships to share costs or to reduce costs by having merchandise or services donated.

Source One: Funding from the Library's Budget

The library contest planner has several decisions concerning how many dollars the library will spend. Most of the decisions are based on the library's size and budget. Small libraries may only have money for personnel and basic operations, so the library budget would not be a source of contest funding. Medium-sized to large libraries may have a marketing budget, but that budget could be already committed. Whether or not the library budget can be a source of contest funding is a local decision depending entirely on local circumstances. There are some low-cost ways of using existing library funds to help underwrite the contest costs. Library merchandise, which is usually obtained at cost, can be used for prizes. Examples of desirable library merchandise include t-shirts, mugs, tote bags, and books. The library may already be paying for the publicity and promotional items from its regular budget. As previously discussed, the contest planner also must determine early how much staff time can be assigned to the contest. This is another cost that can easily be incorporated into the library's current budget. Although rarely is staff added to run a contest, the contest planner should realistically estimate time required for contest activities and obtain the consent of staff and supervisors for their time to be allocated to the contest. If you are planning to incorporate expenses of a library contest into a library's regular budget, make sure to follow the library's budget planning cycle procedures.

Source Two: Funding from the Friends of the Library

Many library contests are partially or totally funded by the Friends of the Library. Individual Friends groups that run gift or book stores are able to provide merchandise from their store or discount coupons or gift certificates for winners to use in the Friends store. This is a win-win partnership as the library has free prizes and the Friends of the Library get publicity and potential new customers.

Friends also can help out with volunteers for the contest recognition event and might have members who have special expertise who could judge a contest.

TIP: When Friends are involved in contest funding, they are more likely to participate in other ways also.

Source Three: Funding from the Library's Foundation

For libraries that have foundations, there are many opportunities for the library contest planner to partner with the foundation on a contest. Foundations often are willing to help get expensive items for prizes from foundation members. Some members give merchandise prize donations from their businesses such as trips or jewelry. Some library foundations are able to give cash prizes for library contests. Foundation members or the foundation itself can also help with financing the recognition event. The Broward County (FL) Public Library Foundation provided the prizes for a summer reading program (see Figure 2-5). This is a great example of how partnerships can enhance your contest.

Figure 2-5. Broward Foundation
Broward County (FL) Public Library Foundation Director
Dorothy Klein shown with summer reading program prize
winners and their families.
(Photo property of Broward County Library Youth Services.)

Source Four: Donations

The majority of library contests have either prizes donated or food or other items for the recognition event donated. Donations can be merchandise, cash, celebrity items, trips, food, drink, tickets, and passes. Before you begin your contest, consider the best places you should approach for donations.

TIP: Look for donations from companies that have a tie to libraries.

TIP: Use your library contest to highlight a unique facet of your community.

Often, new businesses to the area are looking for new customers. Supporting a library contest can provide a new business the solid publicity it seeks. Businesses that are library related often are good places to approach for contest prize donations. Bookstores, computer stores, music stores, and school supply companies are potential donors. The companies that have some tie to the library will be more willing to consider a request because they see the mutual benefits.

Businesses that are related to a contest theme are also possible sources. If the summer reading program's theme is Animal Safari, a zoo, stores that sell stuffed animals, pet stores, or farms might be potential donors. Be sure to ask for animal-related items rather than for the animals themselves. A Reading around the World theme would interest travel supply stores, luggage businesses, international gift stores, and ethnic stores.

Local attractions, movie theaters, local museums, or parks that have an entry fee can be approached for library contest prizes. Consider all the parks and attractions in your local area and start with those that are both very desirable and located within a reasonable distance from the library. Think also of locally produced specialty items such as pickles, chocolates, condiments, popcorn, and snacks, particularly from firms close to the library. Every area, no matter how small, has some area or regional specialty. For example, Hollidaysburg, Pennsylvania, is the home of the Slinky™. An easy contest would be to have a Slinky step challenge or a contest for the most unique Slinky. Spend time thinking about what your library area has that is unique and use it for a theme and try to get the item for a prize.

Local celebrities, sports people, news people, authors, artists, or local officials are also potential prize sources. If you as the contest planner are a new staff member, review with a long-term staff member if any of these people have worked with the library previously. Some people are more willing to work with hometown organizations than others. You want to do some research before approaching individuals for prize donations. Avoid approaching them too frequently and choose the contact person carefully.

Source Five: In-Kind Services

Another way to reduce the costs of the contest is to get donated some service you need to ensure the contest's success. Almost any work that is needed for the contest can be provided by someone outside as an in-kind service. Printing and copying are among the most frequently donated services. The local printing or copying company can print flyers, certificates, posters, bookmarks, and entry and evaluation forms. Trophy companies often donate the engraving on trophies or plaques.

Space is another common type of in-kind donation. In places where the library does not have large general use public spaces, community partners often provide space for exhibits or recognition events. Space in print publications or on broadcasts is also valuable. Local newspapers and radio stations should be approached to sponsor a blog or provide public service announcements and articles about the contest. A local or regional TV station could be approached if there is special interest in the contest. Some schools work with their local media so the winning essay, story, or photograph is published.

When asking for donations of in-kind services, be sure to do your homework first. Make your request fit the capability of the company or organization you are approaching. For example, if you want to ask the local arts center to offer exhibit space and assistance with mounting an exhibit of the winners of your annual photography contest, be sure to check the center's calendar before asking for a specific date that might already be committed to another project. Do not ask a mom-and-pop print shop to provide you with 3,000 brochures printed in full color. Check out what kinds of in-kind services the business may have donated to other community projects. For example, large companies may have in-house printing or marketing capabilities that they would gladly offer as an in-kind service.

There are several ways to approach businesses or organizations for in-kind services. A natural place to start is with businesses the library has had professional relationships with over the years. For instance, if you have all your business cards, brochures, and calendars printed at a particular company, that company might be willing to donate the printing for a smaller project to help you keep costs down. If there is an established relationship, just ask the owner or manager outright for the service. Another approach is to check with your staff to find out if they know people they would be willing to approach for in-kind services. If you do not have any established connections for the service you are seeking, then set aside a day or an afternoon to drive or walk around talking to people in the target businesses. Dress professionally and bring plenty of business cards and materials about the library and the project.

> **TIP:** Over time, careful cultivation of in-kind partners can build into significant partnership relationships with businesses and organizations in the community.

Source Six: Sponsorships

A sponsored contest differs from one in which services or merchandise is donated. In a sponsorship, there is usually higher recognition of the sponsor. Usually, in a sponsored contest, both agencies receive equal billing. An example of the wording used to recognize sponsors would be "The Hometown Public Library and Mary's Dairy Present the Why I Drink Milk Poetry Contest @ the Library." Many sponsored library contests are part of the @ Your Library campaign of the American Library Association (ALA). These national contests are low cost for the individual school or public library because the entry forms are downloadable from the Web or can be filled in online. ALA pays for the design of the contest and the publicity, then finds sponsors to underwrite it. The ALA promotional contest, Major Leagues @ Your Library, had two tickets and travel to the World Series as the grand prize.

> **TIP:** Contests create "buzz" about the library.

Source Seven: Combinations of the Previous Six

When the contest planner is estimating costs for a library contest and is designing the contest, parts of all the funding mechanisms are often used. The longer the planning time, the better the chances of reducing the contest costs by recruiting volunteers to help with looking for in-kind workers and seeking donated prizes and sponsorships.

CONCLUSION

Mapping out the goals for the contest and building a working budget based on those goals is a major step toward creating a successful contest. Making sure goals are clear and well communicated is one of the most important tasks for the contest planner or planning team to address. Although you have established an estimated budget (see Figure 2-6) and contest goals, keep in mind that you will most likely continue to refine them throughout the planning process.

Sample Budget			
	Service/In-kind	Donated Items	Cost
PRINTING Entry forms Flyers Posters Bookmarks Evaluation forms			
ADVERTISING Newspaper PSA TV Billboards In-house calendar/ newsletter			
PRIZES			
STAFF TIME			
RECOGNITION EVENT Certificates Placques/trophies Ribbons Food			
PUBLISHING, PERFORMANCE & EXHIBIT COSTS Exhibit Publication Performance			
TOTALS			

Figure 2-6. Contest Budget Form

Filling out this form can help guide you in your budgeting process.

3 DEFINE THE CONTEST TYPE, AUDIENCE, AND THEME

If carefully made, the decisions in Step Two of the planning process concerning goals and budget will make Step Three—Defining the Contest Type, Audience, and Theme—easier. In fact, making a determination as to the type of contest the team wants to hold, the specific audience the contest will target, and what theme, if any, the contest will follow is a natural extension of the goal-setting and budgeting process. This chapter will examine the three aspects of this planning step in order. However, they are closely intertwined, and the planning team will probably move back and forth among them as this aspect of the contest plan is finalized.

DEFINING THE CONTEST TYPE

The first task in this step is determining what type of contest best fits the goals and budget proposed by the planning team in Step Two. While types of contests will be fully explored later in this chapter, the major categories of contest types to consider at this point are listed here. There may be considerable overlap in these categories (see Figure 3-1). For instance, a naming contest may also help raise awareness of a new library service. It is not necessary for the contest to fit neatly into one category—the categories are simply useful in focusing efforts of those involved in the planning and implementation. Major categories of contest types include the following:

1. Creative—Included here are contests that stress a creative activity, such as a photo, art, or essay contest.
2. Naming—This type includes contests in which the purpose is naming something at the library like a mascot, catalog, or building.
3. Product—This type of contest asks participants to produce a usable library product, such as a logo, bookmark, or signage.
4. Event—This type of contest is when the contest *is* the event, such as summer reading contests and poetry slams.

TIP: A trivia contest in which the answers can only be found on the library's Web site can heighten awareness of a recent Web site redesign.

5. Awareness—Included here are contests that raise awareness of particular aspects or services of the library, like adult reading contests to highlight parts of the collection.

6. General—While it may sound like a catch-all category, the general type of contest in actuality may be made up of a mix of types and purposes and may be aimed at a very general audience. Examples include guessing the number of something or random drawings.

TYPE OF SPONSORING LIBRARY	TYPE OF CONTEST
Public	Summer Reading Bookmark Design Photo Art Trivia Stump the Librarian Poster Dress Up Like Your Favorite Character
Academic	Book Collecting Design Essay or Writing Art Trivia
School Media Centers	"Guess the Number of. . ." Poster Art Coloring Book Selection Design
Special Libraries	Trivia Design Essay or Writing

Figure 3-1. Type of Sponsoring Library/Type of Contest That Can Work Well

DEFINING THE CONTEST SCOPE

Once the team has chosen a general category of type of contest, it is helpful to spend some time considering the scope of the contest. This will help the planner(s) hone in on a specific type of contest to hold. Contest types vary by scope—scope of time, geographic scope, and age scope. Some contests involve entire communities; some even touch the whole nation. Others involve a single department of a library. Library contests are often limited to certain age groups, yet some apply across the board, bringing together people of all ages. The scope of the library contest is determined by the library's need and resources, in other words, the goals and estimated budget established in the previous planning step. For further information on properly scaling the project, see the sections below on how the reach of the contest and the size of the sponsoring library should shape the type of contest that you choose to hold. While there are numerous ways to consider the various types of contests, scope is one of the most important.

Based on the goals and budget established in Step Two of the planning process, the contest planner or planning team can easily identify the scope of the contest. Some clarifying questions can help at this point: Is the contest city-wide or focused on the neighborhoods surrounding a specific library location? Do you hope to involve the whole school or one class or grade? Is the contest part of a larger effort, such as a state or nationwide campaign? How many people are you hoping to involve? Based on answers to questions like these, the team can use the budget and goals to determine if the scope of the contest will be:

- National
- Statewide
- Local
- Online (which may encompass all three of the other levels of scope)

As you move through the next section of this chapter, remember the divisions proposed here are intended to help focus the process for your team, not to limit your creativity. Keep thinking for ways to adapt a particular contest type to the level of scope you and your team have identified as ideal in keeping with the goals and budget you have already established.

> **TIP:** Always think of your contest beyond the moment. You never know what wonderful event may lie just around the next corner!

NATIONAL CONTESTS

National contests have several very clear pluses to them. First, they probably come as a package deal. Since many libraries across the country are offering basically the same thing, there are usually set graphics, press materials, guidelines, forms, and even prizes associated with national contests. This has the added benefit to individual libraries of saving them the time and money of reinventing the wheel. If you choose to participate in such a national program, you will not have to write your own guidelines, make your own entry forms, or write your own press releases. You will not have to figure out what to offer as a prize or how long your contest should last. The contest will come to you prepackaged with these things already decided. Additionally, many national contests have a large prize associated with them for which everyone across the country is competing. This can save you money and time on trying to secure prizes.

> **TIP:** Personalize a national contest to your community by involving a local celebrity or tying it to a popular community festival or celebration.

A good example of national contests are the @ your library contests created by the American Library Association (ALA) as a part of the comprehensive, multi-year @ your library campaign. Free professional graphics for your use are provided by the ALA as part of the Campaign for America's Libraries. These particular graphics are available in many different languages. English, Spanish, and Vietnamese are shown here (see Figures 3-2, 3-3, and 3-4).

Figure 3-2. ALA Reading Logo (English)
(Reproduced by permission of the American Library Association and the Campaign for America's Libraries.)

Figure 3-3. ALA Reading Logo (Spanish)
(Reproduced by permission of the American Library Association and the Campaign for America's Libraries.)

Figure 3-4. ALA Reading Logo (Vietnamese)
(Reproduced by permission of the American Library Association and the Campaign for America's Libraries.)

Many of the @ your library contests will be familiar to you. Join the Major Leagues @ your library was a partnership project between ALA and Major League Baseball. The centerpiece of this information literacy initiative was an online baseball trivia contest. The grand prize winner received a trip for two to a World Series game (see Figure 3-5). First place winners also received prizes. Local libraries promote the campaign to their patrons, and each year, the libraries that brought in the most participants also received various incentives. Trivia questions for the contest were developed by the library staff at the National Baseball Hall of Fame and Museum. The contest was open to all ages, and national participation grew steadily each year.

**Figure 3-5. Join the Major Leagues @ your library®
Grand Prize Winner, Madeline Barnicle, at the World
Series with Billie the Marlin and Sharon Robinson
(As appeared on, and used with permission of, the ALA
Web site.)**

STATEWIDE CONTESTS

Statewide contests are those whose organization involves counties and
communities throughout an entire state. Individual libraries or library systems join with others in participating in the contest, but the major planning

**Figure 3-6. Sasquatch Reading Award Logo
(Courtesy of the Washington Library Media Association.)**

TIP: Use your participation in a statewide contest as a means of networking with your colleagues across the state. Share ideas and strategies and build partnerships for the future.

and organizing are done by a group—usually a state committee or state library organization. Most statewide contests have standardized graphics, press materials, rules, and entry requirements. To participate, libraries must use the same materials as everyone else around the state. They often also require some type of report or end-of-contest evaluation that can be time-consuming to complete, since they almost always focus on numbers—participation rates, circulation, age representation, and other demographic tallies. Like national contests, statewide contests have the main downside of lack of creative control at the local level. However, if you are willing to give up a little control, this aspect of statewide contests can be turned into a plus. Having standardized logos and materials at your disposal means you do not have to allocate valuable staff time and money to creating these pieces of your contest. In some ways, these contests are a ready-to-use package that is often available for individual library use free of charge. Many states contract with nationally known artists for the design of program materials.

Many statewide contests are organized by state library associations. A good example of these is the Best Book contest. Many states hold book selection contests. A nice example of this type of library contest is the annual Sasquatch Reading Award hosted by the Washington Library Media Association (WLMA). The logo for this program is shown in Figure 3-6. Students have to read or have read to them at least two books from the selection list that is available in both a print version and an online version. The selection lists are compiled from nominations made by teachers, students, and librarians. The nominating committee includes librarian representatives from across the state who utilize both their own expertise and input from young readers in developing the annual selection ballot. The selection list targets the intermediate reader in both fiction and nonfiction. Students then use the official ballot to vote on their favorite books. The results are posted on the WLMA Web sites. Each year, the contest draws some 20,000 student participants.*

Other nonlibrary state organizations may sponsor contests to which libraries can connect. When the Kentucky Writers Coalition held its annual Jim Wayne Miller Poetry Contest, for example, a school librarian could have encouraged an entire group or class of students to enter. State education associations, state or regional college and university consortia, and other similar groups also offer good possibilities for libraries to get their patrons involved in statewide contests.

LOCAL CONTESTS

Probably the most common type of contest is the local contest sponsored by individual library systems or even by individual branches or departments within a particular library. The benefits of these contests include the level of control you have over them (in terms of design, scope, and frequency), the ease with which you can tailor them to fit your very specific circumstances (tying them to a specific event at your library), and the sheer variety you can achieve.

There are some downsides to the local contest. For one thing, the entire weight of the project rests on you. The success—or failure—of the project is tied directly to the branch, program, or system that sponsored it. All of the work must be done in-house as well. This means creating or contracting for all your own graphic and publicity pieces, organizing the guidelines and prizes, and recruiting community partners.

> **TIP:** Partner with a local bookstore or bank to make a local contest more manageable.

ONLINE CONTESTS

Many libraries are now sponsoring online contests that are accessed through their Web sites. The beauty of these contests lies in their simplicity and ease of use. Generally, online contests have the following features:

- are inexpensive to design and run
- can be run much more frequently than traditional contests
- are easy to enter and control (may have to supply library card number to enter the contest)

*Washington Library Media Association Web Site: www.wlma.org/Association/sasquatch.htm.

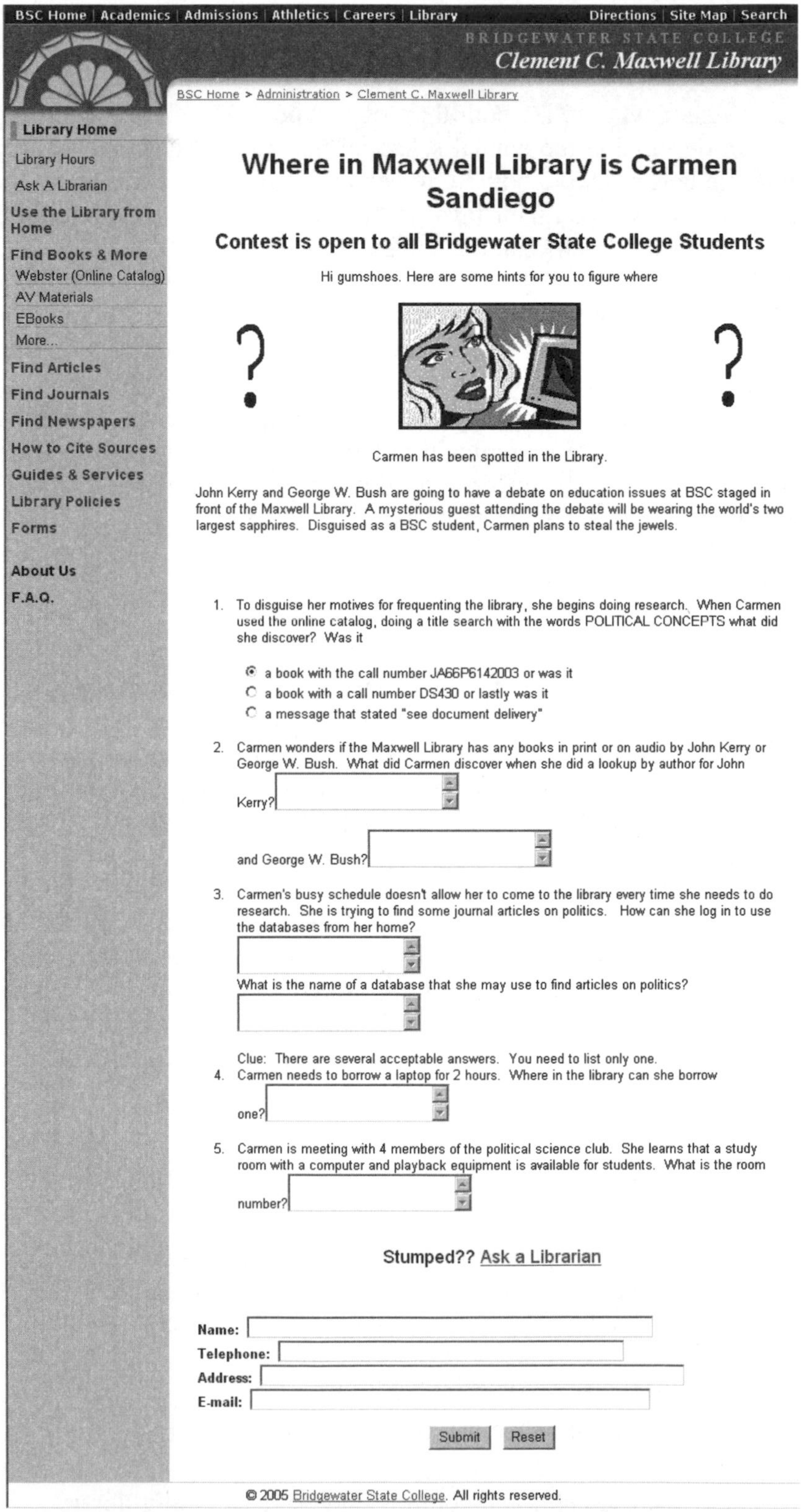

BSC Home | Academics | Admissions | Athletics | Careers | Library   Directions | Site Map | Search

BRIDGEWATER STATE COLLEGE

Clement C. Maxwell Library

BSC Home > Administration > Clement C. Maxwell Library

Library Home
- Library Hours
- Ask A Librarian

Use the Library from Home

Find Books & More
- Webster (Online Catalog)
- AV Materials
- EBooks
- More...

Find Articles
Find Journals
Find Newspapers
How to Cite Sources
Guides & Services
Library Policies
Forms

About Us
F.A.Q.

Where in Maxwell Library is Carmen Sandiego

Contest is open to all Bridgewater State College Students

Hi gumshoes. Here are some hints for you to figure where

? ?

Carmen has been spotted in the Library.

John Kerry and George W. Bush are going to have a debate on education issues at BSC staged in front of the Maxwell Library. A mysterious guest attending the debate will be wearing the world's two largest sapphires. Disguised as a BSC student, Carmen plans to steal the jewels.

1. To disguise her motives for frequenting the library, she begins doing research. When Carmen used the online catalog, doing a title search with the words POLITICAL CONCEPTS what did she discover? Was it
   - a book with the call number JA66P6142003 or was it
   - a book with a call number DS430 or lastly was it
   - a message that stated "see document delivery"
2. Carmen wonders if the Maxwell Library has any books in print or on audio by John Kerry or George W. Bush. What did Carmen discover when she did a lookup by author for John Kerry?
   and George W. Bush?
3. Carmen's busy schedule doesn't allow her to come to the library every time she needs to do research. She is trying to find some journal articles on politics. How can she log in to use the databases from her home?
   What is the name of a database that she may use to find articles on politics?
   Clue: There are several acceptable answers. You need to list only one.
4. Carmen needs to borrow a laptop for 2 hours. Where in the library can she borrow one?
5. Carmen is meeting with 4 members of the political science club. She learns that a study room with a computer and playback equipment is available for students. What is the room number?

Stumped?? Ask a Librarian

Name:
Telephone:
Address:
E-mail:

Submit Reset

© 2005 Bridgewater State College. All rights reserved.

Figure 3-7. Carmen Sandiego Contest Screengrab (Created collaboratively by members of the Public Relations Commitee, November 2004. Reproduced by permission of the Bridgewater State College Clement C. Maxwell Library.)

- create invaluable publicity by increasing Web site traffic and promoting visibility of other library programs and services
- allow a library to have multiple contests running simultaneously to target specific patron groups

Do not let the technical aspects of an online contest discourage you from trying one at your library. Talk to your Webmaster or contact a local computer club for help. Web-based library contests have a downside in that they tend to take the program aspect out of the contest. They also tend to defeat one of the common goals of a library contest, which is to stimulate more traffic into the library buildings. This can be mitigated by creating an online contest that involves use of the library facilities themselves. Bridgewater (MA) State College's Clement C. Maxwell Library did just that with their successful Where in Maxwell Library Is Carmen Sandiego contest. Students entered through the library's Web site, but they had to visit the library to be able to answer the questions for the contest (see Figure 3-7). A big plus of online contests is their appeal to the younger library patron. Today's children and teenagers are used to accessing information via the Internet. It is where they seek answers to their questions for school, entertainment, and communication with friends, relatives, and even teachers. So if you are looking to heighten awareness of library resources among the younger crowd, online contests may be the way for you to go.

CHOOSING A CONTEST TO FIT THE SPONSORING LIBRARY

Not only is scope important when focusing in on the specific type of contest to hold; the planner must also take into account the kind of library sponsoring the contest. The section that follows looks at specific contests that fit well with different kinds of libraries.

PUBLIC LIBRARIES

Probably the most familiar public library contest is the annual summer reading contest. Most public libraries sponsor summer reading programs, and the very nature of the program lends itself to the contest format. Summer reading contests are good examples of contests that do not necessarily have to promote competition at the individual level. Most summer

Figure 3-8. American Girl Party at the Albert L. Scott Public Library in Alabaster, Alabama
This contest encouraged children to dress as their favorite American Girl characters.

reading programs offer prizes and incentives to all the children who participate and complete the program. These types of contests ensure that everyone can be a winner and achieve success. They are great morale boosters for children and parents alike. Often summer reading programs have some aspect that is tied to the state library association, and in this way, you have the best of both worlds. You can make the program fit your

1999 Bookmark
Design Contest
Winner!

Nicole Ronzon

Category

Grades 1 - 3

Celebrating
National Library Week

April 1999

Nicole, a Mandarin Branch customer, was one of 5 bookmark
contest winners.

Jacksonville
Public Library

Figure 3-9. Bookmark:
"Read, Write, and Connect"
(Front)
(Reproduced by permission of
Jacksonville Public Library.)

Figure 3-10. Bookmark:
"Read, Write, and Connect"
(Back)
(Reproduced by permission of
Jacksonville Public Library.)

individual library or department and the particular patron group you serve, but at the same time, many of the graphics, prizes, and press materials are put together by the state library association and made available to everyone.

The possibilities for types of public library contests go far beyond the annual summer reading program. Some possibilities include the following:

- book character look-alike dress-up (Harry Potter and American Girl characters are favorites in this category). See Figure 3-8.
- poster contests
- short story or poetry contests
- read-a-thons
- photo contests
- duct tape contests
- art contests
- trivia contests
- Stump the Librarian contests
- Guess the Number of Library Cards in the Jar contests

Public libraries sponsor contests to design bookmarks, name new spaces in the library (like a new teen reading and study area), create creatures like dragons and other fairy tale creatures, and even design logos for annual reports and new initiatives. In many cases, the contest is one piece of a larger campaign. It is often a fairly easy and inexpensive way to localize any kind of national or statewide event or trend. The Jacksonville (FL) Public Library's 1999 Bookmark Design Contest helped the library celebrate National Library Week. Nicole Ronzon's design, shown in Figures 3-9 and 3-10, won the Grade 1–3 category.

ACADEMIC LIBRARIES

While they may follow the same general formula as other types of library contests, those sponsored by academic libraries, by virtue of the institutions at which they are housed, tend to lean more toward activities that support the postsecondary education experience. Their focus tends toward the scholarly, and the administration of the contest usually involves a variety of campus resources, emphasizing the scholarly expertise so readily available. This can make academic library contests more complicated and time consuming than some of the other types of contests. They also may involve more people, which almost always means more meetings, more discussions, and more opinions, schedules, and needs to accommodate.

These factors need to be taken into account as the planning team moves through Step Five of the planning process, Schedule the Contest.

Because of their tendency toward complexity, academic library contests can produce some end products that have long-lasting benefits for both individual students and the university as a whole. Book collections, branding campaigns, and annual prizes are among the long-term benefits. These contests often have a two-fold purpose—competition among students and increase in awareness and appreciation of scholarly topics or resources.

A hot ticket type of contest for many years at academic libraries has been the book-collecting contest (see Figure 3-11). Students compete to put together an award-winning personal collection of books in a set amount of time. Usually these contests require the student to submit an essay explaining their collection along with a bibliography of the books in the collection. Often these contests have a "celebrity" judge—either an actual celebrity or someone who is a national or international expert of some sort. The winning collections are usually displayed physically in the library or sometimes virtually online. Prizes, ranging from $100 to $1,000, are sometimes awarded, helping to offset the cost of the collecting (see Figure 3-11).

> **TIP:** Involve community and corporate partners in your academic library contest to complement your University's Town-Gown initiatives.

Book collecting contests have been popular at many of the nation's top colleges and universities, from UCLA to Harvard. Some of these contests are administered by library staff, but many are administered by Friends of the Library groups and other volunteers. The special collections departments of academic libraries often play an important role in these contests, which stress the overall learning experience over the competitive nature of the contest. Students are given training and assistance in learning how to collect books and create significant book collections. For instance, an important component of the Robert B. and Blanche Campbell Student Book Collection Competition at UCLA is an annual book collecting workshop where students actually learn how to compete in the contest while gaining valuable information about lifelong book collecting.

Most of the winners of these contests emphasize a theme that tends toward the scholarly. For instance, past winners in the UCLA Campbell Competition, which has been held for more than five decades, have included the Culture of Wine, The Letters and Lives of Oscar Wilde, and Robots in Science Fiction.

Some contests ask for an annotated bibliography of a "wish list" of future additions to the contest. Collections are typically displayed for a period of time after the contest ends. The Slocum Award at Scripps College in Claremont, California, has been recognizing student book collectors since 1936.

Middlebury College Library in Vermont held a unique contest to capitalize on the creative talents of students. Contest entrants were asked to design unique, clear signage for the library (see Figure 3-12).

The Reinert-Alumni Memorial Library at Creighton University in Omaha, Nebraska, sponsors an annual Master of Scholarly Resources Award. The idea behind the contest is to recognize one student each year based on the student's scholarship and writing abilities as evidenced by an essay. The library

Student Book Collection Contest

For University of Minnesota Students

Entry Form

Entry Deadline:
12 noon
Monday, March 7, 2005

This entry form must be accompanied by:

1. A formal annotated bibliography (25 to 50 titles)
2. An essay about the collection (maximum of 1500 words)

Submit entries to:

George Swan
170B Wilson Library
309 19th Avenue South
Minneapolis, MN 55455

Questions?

Contact Elaine Challacombe (612 626-4366; e-chal@umn.edu) or Carol Zinda (612 626-7698; c-zind@umn.edu).

. . . .

Winners will be notified using the information on this form.

Name: ______________________________

Address: ______________________________

City, State, ZIP: ______________________________

Phone: ______________ Email: ______________

Student ID number: ______________

____Undergraduate ____Graduate

College and/or Major: ______________________________

Home Address: ______________________________

City, State, ZIP: ______________________________

Essay title: ______________________________

I give permission to the University of Minnesota Libraries to post my name and excerpts from my winning Student Book Collection Contest entry on the Librariesí web site.

Signature: ______________________ Date: ________

Figure 3-11. University of Minnesota Student Book Collection Contest Entry Form
Universities try to make the entries as easy as possible. For instance, the University of Minnesota's Student Book Collecting Contest has a clear and easy entry form available right on its Web site.
(Reproduced by permission of the University of Minnesota, © Regents of the University of Minnesota. All Rights Reserved.)

Figure 3-12. Poster and Original Artwork Based on the Theme of Popular Apple Ads (Designed by Mark Roark, Middlebury College. Reproduced by permission of Middlebury College.)

advertises the contest by e-mail to the students, in the *Creighton Cornerstone* newsletter, by word of mouth, and in all the academic disciplines. Potential winners must be nominated by a faculty member. Two librarians and two faculty members read all entries, which must show high quality using a variety of sources. The winner of the Master of Scholarly Resources Award is announced at the University President's Honor Banquet and is presented with a check and certificate (see Figure 3-13). The winner is also

Figure 3-13. Sandra Chavez, 2006 Winner of Master of Scholarly Resources Competition (Photo courtesy of Creighton University, Reinhart-Alumni Memorial Library, LaCroix.)

recognized at the banquet, which is attended by the library director. This helps the library meet its goals as well.

Just like contests in other libraries, those sponsored by academic libraries can also just be fun. A good example of this is contests in the mid-1990s put on by the Lewis Music Library at the Massachusetts Institute of Technology. The annual Musician Look-Alike contests were hosted by Captain Hook (of Peter Pan fame), and entrants ranged from Madonna to the Singing Nun.

SCHOOL MEDIA CENTERS

Contests in school media centers are a great way to get students and faculty interested and involved in the library. They are often lighthearted and fun, but the underlying purpose is much more serious. Studies throughout the years have shown a marked connection between reading and academic success. On the plus side for school media specialists, contests that solicit input about book choices from students can really help with collection development and program planning. A possible negative side to school contests is that they can be very program oriented, and this could lead to an overemphasis on programming at the expense of the more traditional uses of the library. Children may begin to view the library as an entertainment vehicle rather than a place for learning and the pursuit of knowledge.

Nevertheless, contests can and have for many years played a valuable role in school libraries, drawing youngsters into the library and investing them with a love of reading and books. In her April 2001 *School Library Journal* article "She's Got a Winner," Janet Woodward talks about how she was able to ignite interest in high school library users through the use of a series of library contests that she says "helped both the faculty and students view the library as a fun, interesting place to be." Her first contest was held around Valentine's Day. Woodward asked twenty teachers to write the title of one of their favorite books when they were in high school on a cut-out Valentine heart. She then pasted the hearts on a bulletin board, along with a list of the teachers submitting titles. Students competed to see who could correctly match the most titles to teachers. About fifty students competed, and even some teachers joined in, although only students were eligible for prizes. A local bookstore donated two $25 gift certificates for prizes.*

In the mid-1980s, the Virginia Educational Media Association's Barbara Booker and Gladys Pannell put together a number of suggestions for staging school library contests sure to please children of all ages. The suggestions range from the simple—Guess the Number of Books in the School Library— to the more involved—Design a 30-second Public Service Commercial to promote use of the school library. Other suggestions include those in which entire classes can participate, like a Decorate Your Door Contest. The class chooses a book together. Then they select a scene from the book. Finally, they decorate the classroom door with the chosen scene.**

> **TIP:** An essay contest in your school media center can generate some excellent writing portfolio pieces for students.

SPECIAL LIBRARIES

Special libraries have wonderful opportunities to sponsor contests connected with their particular missions or area of specialization. The Mary Baker Eddy Library for the Betterment of Humanity in Boston, for instance, has organized a popular contest, Imagine Your Life as a Story in Song. Participants were urged to enter the contest via three possible scenarios. The first was to rewrite lyrics to a song so that they reflected the

---

*Janet Woodward, "She's Got a Winner," *School Library Journal*, April 2001, 43.
**Internet School Library Media Center, "School Library Media Day," http://falcon.jmu.edu/~ramseyil/libslmday.htm.

entrant's life in some way. The second entry option was to write an original set of lyrics to a song in a manner that reflected some pivotal moment or significant aspect of the contest entrant's life. The third option was to put together five or ten existing songs that could form a musical about the entrant's life.

AUDIENCE

The next task in this step of the planning process is specifying the target audience for the contest. Again, the goals and budget from the previous planning step will guide the team in this task. For example, if one of the contest goals is to increase use of a new library service, the planner or planning team needs to think about whom they envision using the new service. Other factors that come into play here include age, amount of time necessary to develop the entry, and how many people in the library's service area might be eligible for the contest. The team should look at several of these factors in more depth as they move through the next steps in the planning process.

Knowing your *target* audience—those people in your community you hope to reach through the contest itself—is an important part of your successful contest. Knowing your audience is integrally tied to many of the other aspects of contests discussed elsewhere in this book, from deciding what type of contest to hold to choosing appropriate prizes and being clear about your goals and plans for the contest. The audience for a contest to promote the launch of your library's new Web site may be very different from the audience for your new adult summer reading program that will run concurrently with the annual children's summer program.

To help you figure out who the target audience is for your particular contest, ask yourself the following questions:

Question One: What does your current library audience look like?—Is your library in an urban, suburban, or rural setting? Are you the only public library in town, or are you one of many branches? Is your campus large or small? What is the ethnic and cultural composition of your school, your campus, or your community? Remember, you do not have to make all these determinations on your own. Enlist the help of the marketing department, other library staff, or Friends of the Library. Talk to staff members who work the circulation desk. Take informal inventories yourself by watching who uses your library at different times of day. This might also be a great partnership activity if you want to enlist a local college marketing class or a public relations firm to do some market research for you.

Question Two: Who *don't* you see in the mix?—If one of your contest goals is to attract new customers, this might be a good group on which to focus your efforts. Visit stores in the library area and observe the people there. Are they the same as or different from the people you see in your own library?

Question Three: Who are some of the potential patrons for your new program, collection, or service?—Perhaps you have just started a new foreign language collection in your library. Think about where you might be able to tap into groups consisting largely of people of other nationalities or ethnicities, such as a Hispanic or Japanese network or the international student association. However, do not limit your thinking here. Consider your community—however you define it for the purposes of your particular library—broadly. Maybe there is a language immersion school nearby. Perhaps a new Japanese factory has moved into your industrial park.

Question Four: What age group are you planning to target?—For example, school libraries may want to open the contest to just one grade rather than the whole school. Public libraries may want to focus contest efforts during the summer so that more kids can enter. However, contests do not have to be limited to a single narrow age category. Many libraries will hold an adult summer reading program along with the children's summer reading program. For instance, the Talking Book Center at the Chicago Public Library runs a summer reading program for adult patrons with vision disabilities. It runs concurrently with the library's children's summer program. Many of the national contests, like Join the Major Leagues@your library, were open to all ages. Targeting a specific age can help in attracting that age group of patrons to the library, but always use the contest opportunity to explore your own creativity. For example, if your children's department has started a new parenting section, you might use a children's contest as an opportunity to promote the parenting section to the adults who bring the children in to register for the contest.

> **TIP:** Always think of contests as a way to promote your library and its unique services.

FOUR POTENTIAL AUDIENCES

One useful way to determine your target audience is to group people by their usage of the library. One possible group is your regular patrons, those who already use the library and library services generally. Many of these will be library card holders. Another group might be termed "nonusers," people in the community who typically do not have library cards. There also are those who do not use their cards regularly. This group of people probably knows about the library and some of its services. They just do not use them. Another group includes newcomers to your community. They have just moved into the community from another city, state, or country. This group may also contain a significant immigrant population, depending on where your library is located. These groups together can be thought of as potential library users or potential new patrons.

There are dangers inherent in grouping people together arbitrarily, but when you are trying to decide what type of contest to hold and what your

> **TIP:** Part of the beauty of library contests lies in their versatility in drawing the interest of a variety of individuals or groups of individuals in the community.

goals are for the contest, it is helpful to know who your audience might be. When your goal for the contest is to market a new library service or to market the library in general as discussed in the first several chapters of the book, it is not just helpful to know who your audience is, it is critical. Looking at these groups individually can help match different types of contests with different types of contest audiences.

Audience 1: General Users (Regular Patrons)

The types of contests that most likely will appeal to your regular library patrons are those that happen on a regular schedule (like annual summer reading contests) and those that introduce or promote a new service, component, or branch of the library. This group of potential contestants is already familiar with and supportive of the library and its programs, so the publicity focus is more on maintaining good customer relations rather than starting them. This contestant group also will be interested in some of the same contests as the nonusers, so be careful not to pigeon-hole them. Do not forget the public relations impact of this group on the larger community. Word-of-mouth advertising is great at any time, but when budgets are particularly strapped, it can be invaluable. If your regular patrons are excited about something going on at the library, it is just about guaranteed that they will share their excitement with their friends, neighbors, and co-workers.

Audience 2: Nonusers

In the group of nonusers, you are likely to find a wide variety of interests on which to base a library contest. As far as the purposes of this book are concerned, successful contests for this category will tend to target people with special interests—writers, artists, trivia buffs, performers, musicians, poets, and video and graphic artists. Your contest goals when targeting these groups could be to increase registered users or card holders or to promote and increase use of a new library service. A contest to design a new library logo, for instance, may have the added benefit of encouraging entrants to look in more depth at your library, since good logos incorporate the spirit and purpose of the organization. If people are looking in more depth at your library, that means they are finding out about your history, special programs, new initiatives and programs, and all the wonderful services and collections you offer.

There are several approaches you and your team can use to involve nonusers in your library contest:

- Make the theme of the contest integrally tied to its purpose. This enhances the promotional aspect of the contest. For example, if one of the goals of the contest is to promote use of the new teen section of your library Web site, you might design a contest that requires teens to use the new Web site to be able to answer questions for the contest. Another excellent example of this can be found in the "Name the" contests. Say your library is trying to come up with a new name for your online catalog. A great way to get community input and build patron ownership of the program is to hold a Name the Online Catalog contest.

- Make signing up for a library card an entry requirement. Often, people do not sign up for a card simply because they think they will never have a use for the library. However, if they actually do have a library card, they may be more inclined to use it. In most cases you can make signing up for a card a quick and easy addition to the contest entry process.

- Make your contest appear to be non–library centered. Sometimes people are put off in some way by the very notion of a library. Maybe they consider themselves non-readers. Maybe they never had any real experiences with libraries growing up. They even may have the notion that libraries are in some way sacrosanct and therefore not welcoming to the average person. The best way around this is to disarm their negative images of the library. A person may not know how to find a book in the library, but he or she may be an excellent photographer. So the desire to enter—and possibly to win—a photo contest may very well override this person's sense that something at the library is not for him or for her. Of course the trick is to keep this person as a patron and regular user once you draw him or her through the doors. In this way, the success of a library contest relies heavily on your entire staff. Make sure everyone knows about the contest, how to enter, and where entry forms are located. Also, make sure your staff is briefed to be extra friendly and accommodating during the course of the contest, aware of the added potential of many new and first-time faces coming through the door.

Audience 3: Newcomers

Newcomers are an audience group that includes transplants to your community from other cities, states, or countries. Obviously, one of your key

TIP: Contests are common in countries throughout the world. They are a good way to build cultural bridges with newcomers to your community.

TIP: Contests can help newcomers become more comfortable with using a library.

goals in targeting a contest toward this group of people would be to heighten general awareness of the library. You also might want to increase circulation or highlight and promote a new or existing library service or section.

It is important with contests targeting this audience that the contest actually gives them something to take away—not just a prize or premium or incentive, but something less tangible yet more meaningful in the long run. For instance, entering the contest, having to interact with library staff, and figuring out how to actually enter the contest might help new immigrants become more comfortable with the idea of free-for-public-use libraries in general. Even signing up for a library card can be a big step, so it may take extra effort to encourage people to register for a contest.

There are several ways to involve newcomers in your library contest. One of the most obvious is to translate materials into different languages. The Weber County (UT) Library System sees a tremendous increase in summer reading participation through the translation of their promotional materials into Spanish (see Figures 3-14 and 3-15). Find out the nationalities of the largest immigrant groups in your community and translate contest promotions and entry forms into those languages. This helps everyone feel more at home, and it ensures everyone understands the process.

Utilize special marketing strategies to reach this specific group. Do not assume your typical marketing tools will work in the same way when marketing to a specific audience. A flyer posted in a strategic location may have much more impact than a display ad in the local newspaper. Grocery stores, restaurants, student union, dorms, beauty parlors, bus shelters, laundromats, and churches are great places to post flyers to market to newcomers in the community. Be sure to ask permission before posting a flyer, even if the area looks like one commonly used for such purposes. You also may want to focus your advertising on alternative print and radio outlets, the college radio station, for instance, or the local Spanish language newspaper.

Design the contest so that it involves the whole family. Relocating to a new community is hard for the whole family, whether it is across the state or across the ocean. Activities that focus on the whole family are more likely to draw people from this audience group to your library. You can design your contest so that there are different age categories for entry. You can also design the contest so that the entire family must collaborate on the entry. For instance, in 1999, the Schaumburg Township District Library in Illinois held an essay contest titled What My Library Means to Me. Adults and kids from across the community sent in essays, which were then submitted to the Illinois State Library. Two essays were chosen to appear in a special report, "What My Library Means to Me: A Special Report in Honor of the Library of Congress Bicentennial."*

A photo contest can offer participants (whether newcomers or long-time

*Audrey Fischer, "A National Celebration: Library's Bicentennial Reaches Across the Nation," *The Library of Congress Information Bulletin*, August–September 2000, http://www.loc.gov/loc/lcib/00089/celebration.html.

DE CHINCHE POR LOS LIBROS

El Sistema de Bibliotecas del Condado de Weber
Programa de Curso de Verano para Niños 2004

Acompáñanos para ocho semanas de lectura divertida en cada una de las bibliotecas. El registro empieza el **primero de Junio**. ¡Todos los eventos son **gratuitos!** Los niños de tres años en adelante disfrutarán más de este programa. Los premios de los sorteos semanales donados por negocios locales empezarán el 12 de Junio. Para más información, favor de llamar a 337-2639.

 **Bibliotecas** SISTEMA DE
DEL CONDADO DE WEBER

Biblioteca Principal
2464 Jefferson Ave Ogden,
UT 84401   801-337-2639

lunes–jueves	10 a.m.–9 p.m.	**Sucursal Norte**	**Sucursal Valle de Ogden**	**Sucursal Suroeste**
viernes y sábado	10 a.m.–6 p.m.	475 E 2600 N	131 S 7400 E	1950 W 4800 S
domingo (set.–mayo)	1 p.m.–5 p.m.	Ogden, UT 84414	Huntsville, UT 84317	Roy, UT 84067
		801-782-8800	801-745-2220	801-773-2556

2004

**Figure 3-14. Go Buggy over Books (Spanish)
(Permission to reprint granted by Weber County Library
System.)**

Join us for eight weeks of reading fun at every library location. Registration begins June 1. All events are free! Children aged three and older will most enjoy this program. Weekly drawings for prizes donated by local businesses will begin on June 12. For more information, please call 337-2639.

Main Library
2464 Jefferson Ave Ogden,
UT 84401-2404   801-337-2639

Hours
Mon. – Thurs. 10am–9pm
Fri. – Sat.   10am–6pm
Sun. (Sept.–May) 1pm–5pm

North Branch
475 E 2600 N
Ogden, UT 84414
801-782-8800

Ogden Valley Branch
131 S 7400 E
Huntsville, UT 84317
801-745-2220

Southwest Branch
1950 W 4800 S
Roy, UT 84067
801-773-2556

2004

Figure 3-15. Go Buggy over Books (English) (Permission to reprint granted by Weber County Library System.)

residents) a chance to explore their community. My Brooklyn, a photo and essay contest sponsored by Brooklyn Public Library and Con Edison, captures the beauty and complexity of the borough through the eyes and imaginations of its residents (see Figure 3-16). Their words and images reveal what unites Brooklyn and what makes the community unique—its beauty and blight, its history and edge, its toughness and diversity—but most of all, its pride. Winners are chosen based on originality and the ability to capture the spirit of Brooklyn. The winners from three different age categories are exhibited in the Central Library Grand Lobby.

Make sure the contest requires skills and knowledge that anyone could have, not just those living in your city or town. The surest way to turn people away from your contest is to have a contest that asks entrants to answer questions you assume everyone should know but that they have no knowledge of whatsoever. Instead, use those types of questions as learning opportunities for newcomers. You can probably even come up with a creative way to work the act of finding the answers into the contest itself.

Figure 3-16. My Brooklyn Photo Contest Finalist
("Images of Coney Island." Photograph by Nehru KeLevh,
taken August 30, 2005.)

Audience 4: Constant Contestants

The last group of potential entrants to your contest is by no means the largest, but it still must be considered when designing your contest. This group can be termed the "constant contestants." These are folks who, quite simply, like to enter contests. Maybe they enjoy the competition. Perhaps they like winning prizes. Regardless of the reason, they tend to enter every contest they come across, whether it is a sweepstakes from a fast food company or an online pop-up window contest to win a new computer or a trip to the Bahamas.

TIP: Constant contestants may become new library users.

How can this group fit into the overall promotional plan of your contest? Everyone is a potential new patron, and chances are, this is a largely untapped group in your community. So seize the opportunity the contest affords you to tap them. One way to do this is to show them why they need the library. Perhaps during the contest period, you can make sure there are prominent and visible displays of books and periodicals and even lists of Web sites relating to contests in general.

By taking the time first to examine who is currently using and who is not using your library, you can then take that information to begin painting a picture of your target audience. When you are doing this, try to think both of whom you would like to see entering the contest and also whom you would like to see using the new service or equipment or branch your contest may be promoting. If you and your staff or contest team are having a tough time envisioning the target audience in general, sometimes it is helpful to find a picture of or actually describe a typical member of this audience. Personalizing the audience in this way makes it easier for everyone to think concretely about how the contest can work, how to promote it, and how specifically to tie it into whatever event or service it is trying to promote.

Finding out who your audience is and might be is one of the most fun and most useful aspects of contest planning. It gives you a chance to show your creativity and think about your patrons and customers in different ways.

THEME

Once the type of contest and the target audience have been determined, the final task in this step in the planning process is making a decision about whether or not to use a theme for your contest. Some contests have themes. Others do not. The decision about whether or not to use a theme is most often a practical one. For simpler contests, like random drawings or "guess the number of " contests, the extra time and expense of using a theme simply is not justified. It really will not add any measurable value to the contest. Larger and more complex contests—for example, those involving multiple sites or partners—usually benefit most from the use of a theme. That is because the theme can serve as a good focal point for those even peripherally involved. The most familiar themes often center on the National Library Week theme or the Summer Reading Program theme.

With a themed contest, all of the materials and the prize(s) usually are centered on a single central idea or organizing principle. If the contest was to write an essay, "The Book That Most Influenced My Life," for example, the design of the entry form would have books on it, all of the promotional items would contain the book theme, and the prize might be an autographed book. The theme can be the one idea that draws all the parts of the contest together into a concerted whole. The Ann Arbor (Michigan) District Library held a summer reading program for all ages that had a Southwestern theme. The younger readers' program was called Catch a Desert Dream, and the Young Adult/Adult program "for Summer Readers 14 to 140" was called Readers of the Purple Sage. The publicity and registration materials, as well as the reading logs, all cleverly incorporated the desert southwest feel through the use of colorful graphics and recycled paper that resembled sandstone (see Figure 3-17).

Contest themes can be very useful to arouse the enthusiasm and convey the idea that the contest is well conceived. Often the contest themes are connected to current events, for example, upcoming elections or even sporting events like the Kentucky Derby. Connecting to a popular event provides a sound basis upon which to build the contest promotion. Although current events provide sound themes, be careful not to go overboard in relating to the theme. Carried too far, themes can easily degenerate. For example, requiring staff members to decorate an area promoting the contest theme, dress thematically, and operate in character for the duration of the contest period may lead to staff dissatisfaction and be over the top. Staff might see this as extra work that fails to increase participation in the contest or long-term public interest. Also, overzealous pursuit of a theme might appear ridiculous to outside observers.

Other successful contest themes may be descriptive of one or more of the objectives the library wants to achieve by use of the contest. A

Figure 3-17. "Readers of the Purple Sage" Materials (Reproduced by permission of the Ann Arbor (MI) District Library.) (*Continued on page 59*)

Instructions

1. Register at the Main Library Fiction & Media Desk or at any Branch Library Reference Desk. You may keep this reading record at the Library or take it home.

2. Begin at any designated Southwestern site.

3. Read one of the designated genres at each site you choose.

4. Select 6 titles and record your selections in the space provided.

5. Try to read a variety of genres.

6. After reading 6 books, readers will receive a $3.00 discount coupon at **Nicola's Books, A Little Professor Bookstore**. Young Adults (ages 14-18) who read 6 books will also receive a coupon for a free video from **Hollywood Video**.

Readers will also be eligible for a drawing for other prizes donated by the following local merchants:

> **Banditos California Style Restaurant**
> **Barnes & Noble Booksellers**
> **Borders Books & Music**
> **Bruegger's Bagels**
> **Jim Schulz - Potter**
> **Michigan Theater**
> **Prickly Pear Southwest Café**
> **Saguaro Rare Plant Nursery**
> **Tios Restaurant**
> **University Musical Society**
> **Whole Foods Market**

Name _____

Address _____
_____

Phone _____

School & Grade _____ Branch _____
(if applicable)

	Genre	Author/Title
1		
2		
3		
4		
5		
6		
7		
8		
9		
10		
11		
12		
13		
14		
15		

Ann Arbor District Library
343 S. Fifth Avenue, Ann Arbor, MI 48104
734.327.4200

Sponsored by the Friends of the Ann Arbor District Library 6/99

Figure 3-17. "Readers of the Purple Sage" Materials (Reproduced by permission of the Ann Arbor (MI) District Library.) (*Continued on page 60*)

Figure 3-17. "Readers of the Purple Sage" Materials
(Reproduced by permission of the Ann Arbor (MI) District Library.) (*Continued on page 61*)

Figure 3-17. "Readers of the Purple Sage" Materials (Reproduced by permission of the Ann Arbor (MI) District Library.) (*Continued on page 62*)

Figure 3-17. "Readers of the Purple Sage" Materials
(Reproduced by permission of the Ann Arbor (MI) District Library.) (*Continued from page 61*)

contest to name a library product is an example of this. The library gets a new name for its product or service without having to incur costs of a public relations firm, and at the same time it gets publicity for the library.

There is no limit for the selection of appropriate contest themes, but the selected theme should always (1) be realistic in describing the contest and (2) appeal to the potential contestants as descriptive of a task to be accomplished rather than the basis for a childish game. Put on your creative thinking cap and theme away. Also, online, check WebJunction (www.webjunction.org)

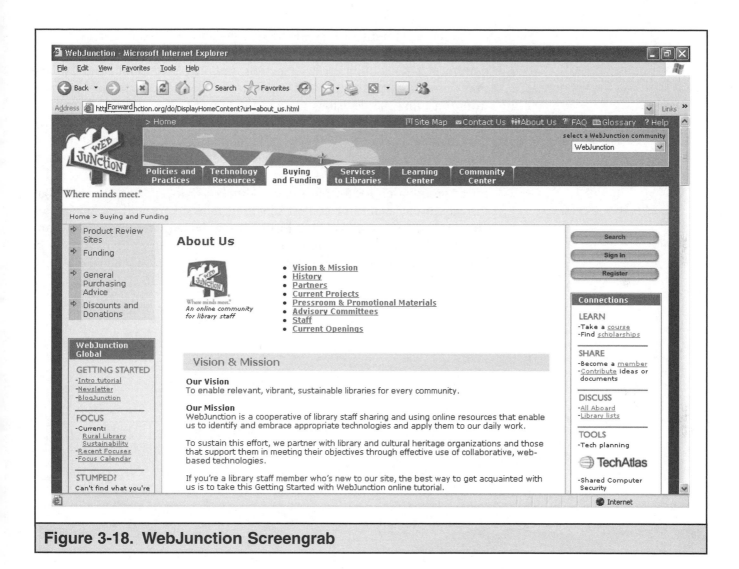

Figure 3-18. WebJunction Screengrab

and find recent, creative, successful library contest themes. WebJunction is a great place to connect with others in the library world (see Figure 3-18).

CONCLUSION

Completing Step Three in the planning process, Defining the Contest Type, Audience, and Theme, helps the planning team get to the heart of the contest. A clear picture of the contest begins to emerge. The contest planner knows exactly what and whom the contest will involve. It is now time to get to the nuts and bolts of how the team's vision can become a reality. The next steps in the planning process examine specifics of contest entry requirements, scheduling, prize selection, judging, promotion, and evaluation. In each of these steps, it is critical for the contest planners to keep firmly in mind the decisions already made in Steps Two and Three. The goals and budget have helped determine the type of contest that will be held and the specific audience being targeted. In turn, the contest type and audience have helped the team decide on whether or not to use a theme and if so, what theme to use. While the steps in the planning process follow a linear progression for the purposes of this book, always keep in mind that the day-to-day reality of contest planning most likely will include a fair amount of movement back and forth among the steps as the specifics are refined. Use the plan and the planning process to keep everyone on track, but do not be afraid to continue to make adjustments along the way.

4 DETERMINE ELIGIBILITY CRITERIA AND RULES

Now that you have the contest planner or team on board, have selected the partners and contest goals, and have decided the budget, contest type, audience, and theme, the next step is determining the eligibility criteria and rules.

DETERMINE ELIGIBILITY FACTORS

There are five main eligibility factors that will have an effect on your contest, and each one needs to be carefully considered. Make sure that you discuss each factor thoroughly, as your decision about each one may significantly change the number of contest participants. Since you have already reviewed the goal-setting section of this book, you will understand the strong connection between the goals of the contest and the eligibility requirements. If your goal is to increase visits to the Web site by nine- to fifteen-year-olds, the only people eligible for your Web site quiz contest would be nine- to fifteen-year-olds. This is where being clear about your target audience (which you defined in Step Three) really comes into play. Once the age has been determined, you need to decide if it was your goal to reach nine- to fifteen-year-old library card holders or all nine- to fifteen-year-olds living within your service area, or all nine- to fifteen-year-olds who use your Web site. You can see by this example that when you are setting your eligibility requirements, you must consider at least these five factors for every contest you hold:

AGE

What is the target age of the contest participants? Is the contest for all ages or for some age segment? Will the contest goals and theme work for all ages or only a specific age group? For some contests, age is irrelevant, and for other contests, it is very important. You might even segment the group of entries by age and have different age-appropriate prizes. A contest to guess the number of bricks to be used in a new building project could be open to any age. Art or literature contests are often divided into age categories.

CARD HOLDERS

Should you restrict the contest only to people who are current card holders? Should you make eligible all who apply for and are eligible for a card during the contest eligibility period? Is there some valid reason to restrict the contest to only people who meet the eligibility requirements for cards? If you are trying to increase library usage as your contest goal, you should not restrict the contest to library card holders. However, if you live in an area with no reciprocity among either cities or corner-touching state areas, you might want to limit the contest to card holders. Careful adherence to your contest goals and commitment to your target audience will be your best guide when considering this factor.

LIVE IN DISTRICT OR AREA

Should the contest be limited by geographic boundaries? What is the rationale for making this restriction? Are you on a county or state boundary that might severely impact this criterion? Large city libraries or libraries with large multicounty service areas often limit the contest to their areas. They limit it because they know that they could not handle the volume of entries if there were no service area limit.

OPEN TO ANYBODY

Some library contests do not have boundary or card-holding restrictions. They are open freely to anybody who chooses to enter. As people from all over the world use local libraries' Web sites, they see the information about contests posted on the sites. Before the Web and worldwide connectivity, this was not a factor you would have needed to take into account. Today it is a factor for serious consideration.

GROUP OR INDIVIDUAL

In some contests it is important to specify whether only an individual can enter or whether it is okay for a group to make an entry. Many library users are comfortable with working collaboratively and only would be comfortable making a group entry. The contest planner needs to decide whether the contest is open only to individuals or if groups may develop a contest entry.

Make sure a statement about group or individual entry acceptance is included on the entry form.

MAKING THE ELIGIBILITY DECISION

Take time to weigh the pros and cons of each eligibility factor. Sometimes other departments should be consulted before the final decision is made. Decisions the planning team has already made about goals, scope, and intended audience play a key role as well at this stage in the planning process. If a contest attracts 500 card-holder entries but has the potential to draw in 2,000 entries if it is open to anyone in the service area or 10,000 if there are no boundary restrictions, the escalating number of entries would have a significant impact on the staff assigned to collect the entries, on the judges, and on all other staff connected with the contest. Time spent in determining clear and appropriate eligibility criteria will help avoid questions and problems later in the contest.

WRITING THE CONTEST RULES

A key consideration in designing a successful contest is setting up clear entry rules and designing an entry form. Again, moderation is important. The rules should be comprehensive enough to generate the types of entries you and your team are envisioning as well as to make it easy for all potential contestants to understand. On the other hand, they should not be so detailed that people will not read them. For most contests, you should be able to summarize the rules on a single 8½×11 inch sheet of paper or less.

> **TIP:** Entry rules should be simple.

In order to have clear entry rules, consider what questions potential entrants might have, as well as the information and type of entry the planning team would like to see. You may have some additional rules that are unique to your specific contest, but most contest rules would include the following items:

1. Define what constitutes the entry. Included in this area should be any physical descriptions. These could include the size of the paper for submittal and number of words for a submission. For art work, this section should include

what dimensions are acceptable, whether or not the piece should be matted or framed, or whether a digital image is acceptable. If it is a photograph, can it be black and white or color, computer generated, or computer altered?

2. Determine how many entries are allowed. Many contests allow only a single entry. If you have a single entry rule, can you develop an easy way to sort out multiple entries? Some contests limit not only the number of entries per individual but also the number of entries per family. That is a limitation that is very hard to determine because many family members have different last names.

3. Set the age requirements. The type of contest often sets the age rule. The fewer the number of age categories, the less time spent on separating the entries for the judging.

4. State the contest start and finish dates, including time of day for deadline.

5. Identify where the entry form should be delivered or turned in. Decide the place or places entries should be submitted. If the entries are to be submitted only online, make provisions to let those entrants without computers submit their entries on a library computer. Decide if the entry can be returned in the bookdrop or not. If you allow the bookdrop as an entry point, set a time and date on those submittals, too.

6. Outline who can participate according to your previously determined eligibility criteria.

Your contest goal plays a major role in setting entry rules. Every contest may have some rules that are unique to the particular contest. If the goal is to promote your new reader advisory service, then you need to build a trial of the service into your rules. In other words, to enter the contest, the entrant will have to use the reader advisory service. If the goal is to bring more people into the library, then you need to require entrants to visit a library location. This could be a rule as simple as having to pick up an entry form or turn in an entry at the library itself. The Ela Area Public Library in Lake Zurich, Illinois, encouraged people to visit the library with its Fall into Books reading promotion that utilized a clever instant winner card (see Figure 4-1). People received a prize just for coming into the library, and there were additional incentives for new patrons. If you want to generate large community participation, make the entry something simple, like a question for a Stump the Librarian contest or a suggested name for your Web page or new browser.

Figure 4-1. Ela Area Public Library Contest Materials (Image Courtesy of Ela Area Public Library.)

Figure 4-1. Ela Area Public Library Contest Materials (Image Courtesy of Ela Area Public Library.) (*Continued on page 70*)

Figure 4-1. Ela Area Public Library Contest Materials (Image Courtesy of Ela Area Public Library.) (*Continued from page 69*)

DESIGNING THE ENTRY FORM

After you have determined contest eligibility and established the basic rules, you need to design the entry form. Most entry forms are one page or less. A good contest has a well-defined and easy-to-understand entry process. This may take the form of a simple, tear-off submission slip (see Figure 4-2) or a single sheet (see Figure 4-3).

Whatever entry forms are required, they need to be available in good supply at all participating library and community locations. If your community has a significant population of non–native English speakers, you may need to consider translating your materials into other languages to achieve full accessibility for your patrons. If a fee is associated with entry, it needs to be clearly stated in all materials relating to the contest so no one is taken by surprise. You also need to state whether or not the contest is open to everyone or limited by age, by whether they have a library card, or by whether they live in your service area. You may want to post the entry form and guidelines on your Web site for easy access.

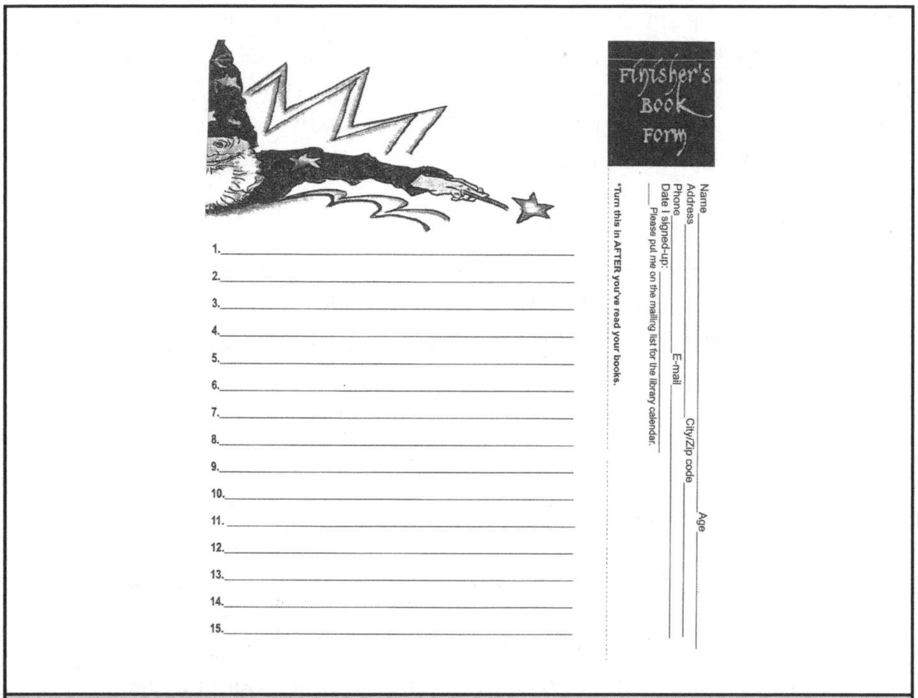

Finisher's Book Form

Name ______ Age ______

Address ______ City/Zip code ______

Phone ______ E-mail ______

Date I signed-up: ______

___ Please put me on the mailing list for the library calendar.

*Turn this in AFTER you've read your books.

1. ______
2. ______
3. ______
4. ______
5. ______
6. ______
7. ______
8. ______
9. ______
10. ______
11. ______
12. ______
13. ______
14. ______
15. ______

Figure 4-2. Tear-Off Entry Form

Main Street Public Library Prettiest Pet Contest
Entry Form

NAME: ______

ADDRESS: ______

______

CITY: ______ STATE: ______ ZIP: ______

DAYTIME PHONE: ______

EVENING PHONE: ______

E-MAIL ADDRESS: ______

IF UNDER AGE 18, PLEASE HAVE A PARENT OR GUARDIAN SIGN HERE: ______

NAME OF PET: ______

BRIEF DESCRIPTION OF PET: ______

PLEASE TAPE OR PASTE A PICTURE OF YOUR PRETTY PET HERE (photos will not be returned):

Please drop your entry at the Main Street Public Library, III Main Street, by the close of the contest, May 18 at 5 P.M. Winners will be announced at the Annual Main Street Public Library Pet Fair on May 24.

Figure 4-3. Full-Page Entry Form

Entrants need to know if their submissions must be made in person or if they can be mailed or e-mailed to the library. They also need to know if their entries will be returned (which is particularly important when dealing with written or art work) and where and when they need to pick them up or if they will be returned by mail. Figure 4-4 offers some sample entry guidelines.

Guidelines for the Annual Young Writers Short Story Contest

First Place

$50 cash prize, along with publication in the *Sun-Times*

Honorable Mention

Two $25 cash prizes, along with publication in the *Sun-Times*

Submission Guidelines

The contest is open to all writers age 18 and younger living in Central City
Each writer may submit 1 short story free of charge
Additional stories may be submitted for a fee of $3 each
All entries must be typed with 12 point plain typeface. Two copies of each story must be submitted, with the entrant's name, address, and phone number appearing on one copy only. No work will be returned. Winner will be announced at the Awards Ceremony on February 23, at 7 PM in the Central City Public Library board room.

Submission deadline is January 31

You can bring your story to the Library during regular operating hours (do not put any entries in the book drop!). Or you can mail your entries to the Library:

Short Story Contest
Central City Public Library
1234 Main Street
Central City, NY 10000

Figure 4-4. Sample Entry Guidelines

Some library contests have the entry form, the rules, and everything a person needs to know about the contest together on a single page. The Johnson County Library in Overland Park, Kansas, Bookmark Contest entry form is a good example. An interesting aspect of this entry form is that participants actually drew their bookmark designs on the entry form itself, saving paper and time (see Figure 4-5). The form clearly identifies age divisions for entry and offers a description of the contest. In addition to acknowledging the sponsor, Friends of Johnson County Library, the entry form also offers a check box for people to receive more information about the Friends.

National Library Week 2006 Bookmark Design Contest

Best Friends Forever

Sponsored by Johnson County Library and the Friends of Johnson County Library

Get out your colored pencils, markers, crayons, fingerpaints or watercolors and show us how the library is your FRIEND! Make it colorful!

In honor of the 50th anniversary of the Friends of the Library, design a bookmark showing how the library is your friend; how the library has helped you; how librarians are your friends; or how you can be a friend to the library. Then tell us in a few words why the library is your friend or how you can be a friend to the library.

Return this entry form to any Johnson County Library location by April 30, 2006. Winners will receive gift certificates from the Friends of the Library and have their creations reproduced on bookmarks distributed in the libraries. All designs become the property of the Johnson County Library and cannot be returned.

CATEGORIES: *(Please check one)*

❑ Preschool-Kdg.   ❑ Grades 7-8

❑ Grades 1-2   ❑ Grades 9-12

❑ Grades 3-4   ❑ Adults, ages 18 and up

❑ Grades 5-6

Please print the following information:

Name _____

Address _____

City _____ State _____ Zip _____

Phone Number _____

❑ Please send our family more information on the Friends of the Library.

Please tell us how the Johnson County Library is your friend or how you can be a friend to the library:

_____

_____
(Use back side of entry form if necessary)

For children only:

Age _____ Grade _____

School _____

Figure 4-5. Johnson County Bookmark Contest Form (Used by Permission of Johnson County Library.)

All contest forms should include the following items:

1. The name of the contest and a brief description
2. The eligibility criteria
3. The rules
4. Information about the prizes
5. When the winners will be selected and the method
6. Information about partners and sponsors
7. When the prizes will be awarded
8. Name, address, and phone number of the library

The Mount Prospect Public Library in Illinois used an unusual approach in their adult summer reading program brochure. Not only did they include information about the contest rules, prizes, and sponsor, they also included information about other concurrent library programs. The inside of the brochure served as the entry form. It was all contained on a double-sided 11 × 17 inch folded page (see Figure 4-6). One of the outstanding features of this brochure is recognition of Outback Steakhouse®, which donated fifty grand prizes. Each of the winners received a lunch for four at the Outback Steakhouse in Schaumburg, Illinois. Figure 4-6 is another example of an entry form that is clear and easy to understand.

Some library contest planners develop a contest information sheet in addition to the entry form and rules. This sheet gives additional information from the entry form and may contain some of the eight basic elements from the entry form on this sheet instead. It is easier for both the entrants and the staff to have everything all together, but the individual type of contest dictates what printed information works best.

The contest rules also must articulate clearly the way in which the winning decision will be made. Will the winning contest entries be decided based on merit, consensus, vote, a predetermined ranking scale, creativity, chance, blind ranking, or some other method? It is very important that the potential contest entrant fully understand the rules, including how the contest will be judged.

A good example is the list of rules developed for the weekly drawings in the Read Your Way West adult summer reading program at the David A. Howe Public Library in Wellsville, New York:

1. Read any books of your choice. Submit an entry form for each book. Place entry forms in box located at the reading program display near main desk at the library.
2. Library staff will draw a winner each Monday. Staff will call winners and post their names. To qualify, you must have a current library card. The library staff will

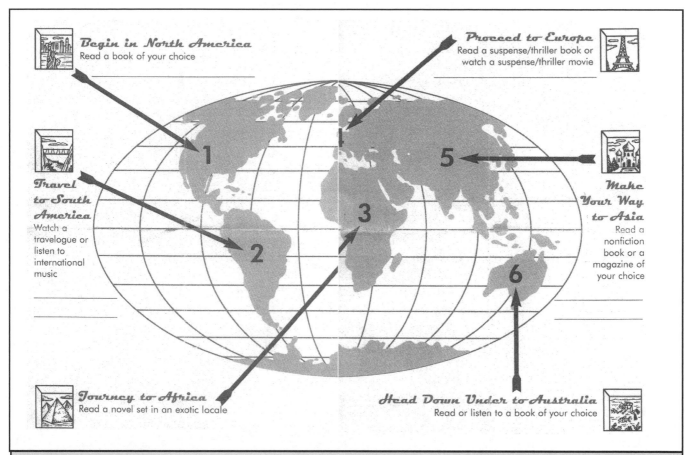

Figure 4-6. Mount Prospect Entry Form
The Amazing Reading Race Adult Summer Reading program entry form utilized colorful graphics, good sponsor recognition, easy-to-understand rules, and other key information. A portion of the entry form is pictured here.
(Used by permission of Mount Prospect Public Library.)

gladly update your card or issue a new card. Library cards are free.

3. Prizes must be picked up by September 5, 2005.

Another contest piece that is often included in library contests is a tip sheet for entrants about how they can win. The next section of this chapter goes into more detail about creating a tip sheet, which is a set of guidelines to help a person enhance his or her chances of success in the contest.

TIP SHEETS FOR CONTEST ENTRANTS

How can I win? This is a question every contest planner and organizer hears over and over. Of course, you cannot directly answer the question, but you can give advice on items that will help all contestants. Entries that follow the rules also will make the contest judge's job easier. As the person holding the contest, your job will be easier if you adapt from the following guidelines a one-page list of ideas relevant to your contest. Then, make copies and have them ready when you hear the question, "But how do I win?"

After you review this general list, you might want to add some helpful ideas specific to your contest. For instance, you might include a short bibliography of helpful reference materials, databases, and even a Webography. It is not the contest planner's job to provide all of the paths for the contest entrant but rather to provide general pointers to avoid having to answer repetitive questions that all contest entrants might have. A question-and-answer sheet about the contest could be included with the entry blank.

What are some of the areas to be included in the tip sheet? Information about following the rules, neatness, timeliness, and creativity are four main areas.

FOLLOWING THE RULES

One might think it redundant to have contest rules and then have to remind people to follow them, but almost every contest has entries that are disqualified because the rules were not followed. Stress the importance of following every rule, not just the rules that the contest entrant thinks are the most important. Stress that the rules are not optional and that entries containing exceptions—no matter how worthy the reasons—will not be considered. The more specific the entry rules, the more questions the people who run the contest will have to field. Consider this when establishing the contest rules. In order to have a successful contest and satisfied entrants and winners, you should allow no exceptions to the rules. If you allow one exception, you will need to consider others. Soon the rules mean little. The contest judges will have a very difficult time in selecting winning entries. A successful contest encourages all the contest entrants to follow all the contest rules exactly.

If the contest has set numbers for any part of the contest, stick to the numbers. If two photos are the limit, do not accept four. If a writing contest has a one-page limit, do not accept three pages. A gentle but firm rejection usually allows the entrant to understand they must follow the rules.

If the contest planner has determined to limit the number of entries per person to one or any other specific number, the planner must determine ahead of time how this will be monitored. Some contests do not limit the number of entries because it is more work to determine if the limit was subscribed to rather than deal with a few more entries.

The area in which entrants most often ask for exceptions is with age limits. Parents often ask for exceptions when their child is only a month or even a few days away from the specified age limits. This is particularly true when the prizes increase in value for the older age categories. When considering what prizes to give for different age groups, pick age-appropriate prizes but try to keep the prizes fairly equal in monetary value so parents and children will not be tempted to request a move to another age group. It is a part of human nature that people will ask for exceptions. You cannot stop the asking, but you can tell the staff likely to get the questions to be ready to politely and firmly say, "I'm sorry, but there are no exceptions."

NEATNESS OF THE ENTRY

Neatness of an entry cannot be stressed enough. Regardless of the type of entry or the age of the entrants, this can be the key factor in selecting a winner. Unreadable forms cannot be used. Stress to participants the importance of filling out entry forms legibly (see Figures 4-7 and 4-8).

Whether it is test-taking, preparing a job application, filling out college application forms, or completing any other piece that requires clarity and readability, teachers and employers have always stressed that neatness counts. The same is true for contest entries. If a judge cannot clearly read the entry, if there are mistakes in grammar, smudges on photographs, or mussed corners on art work, a judge will quickly put those entries in the non-winner pile. Suggest to the entrants that they think like a contest judge would think about their entries. If the judge had already judged fifty neat, clean entries and then came upon a messy one, it probably would not receive much more than a quick glance. Neatness does count, even if it is not specifically stated on the entry form.

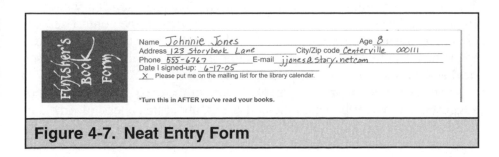

Figure 4-7. Neat Entry Form

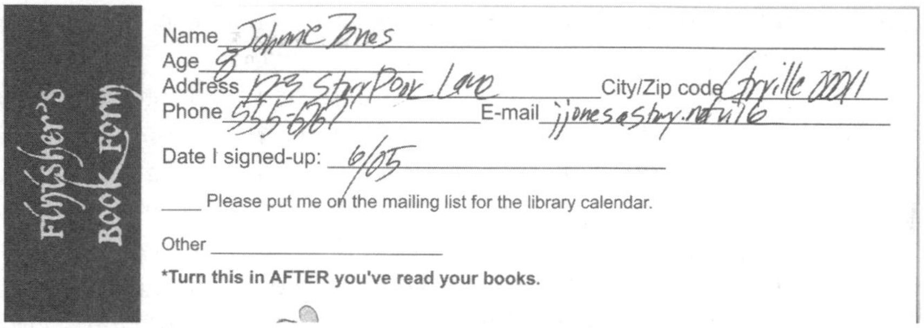
Flyisher's Book Form

Name
Age
Address City/Zip code
Phone E-mail
Date I signed-up: 6/05

___ Please put me on the mailing list for the library calendar.

Other

*Turn this in AFTER you've read your books.

Figure 4-8. Messy Entry Form

TIMELINESS

Contest organizers will hear many creative reasons why an entry could not be turned in on time. Again, this is not an area in which to make exceptions, because if one exception is made for an entry that is only one day late, who will determine how late is too late to turn in entries? Remember to specify the place to which the entries should be returned. If not, you will receive one or two in the after-hours bookdrop. Specify if the entries must be returned to a specific place rather than having to determine later whether or not to accept the bookdrop entries that were probably put in after closing hours. The time deadline should be set at closing time of the contest end day. If the end time is 5 P.M. on a day that the library closes at 9 P.M., you will have to make decisions concerning the entries turned in at 5:05 P.M., 5:10 P.M., and 5:15 P.M. because the person's clock was slow. If the building is closed, you reduce the problem questions about late entries.

CREATIVITY

One of the reasons to hold a library contest is to stimulate and reward creativity. Challenge the library staff to develop some ideas that would help stimulate either children's or adults' creativity in a specific library contest. Engage staff who have an interest in or are experts in the contest subject area to help with suggestions. Some libraries hold a class on the topic area in the months prior to a contest. An example of this is photography classes held at the library prior to the photography contest.

In contests for children, the level of work of the entry might lead you to suggest that a parent prepared the entry. Talk about this ahead of time and determine how this situation will be handled. Schools have a similar challenge with science fair entries. Youth services staff members need to emphasize the fun of the contest over the competitiveness. Many contests for children have a small prize for all entrants and then a random drawing for larger prizes. At the Broward County Library in Ft. Lauderdale, Florida, all children who participate in the summer reading program receive prizes for reading. Then, all those who complete the program become eligible for a drawing for a computer and printer (see Figure 4-9).

> **TIP:** Remember to KISS— Keep It Simple, Silly!

Figure 4-9. Broward County Library Summer Reading Contest Winners
(Photo property of Broward County [FL] Library Youth Services.)

Figure 4-10 is a sample checklist for contest entrants that can be adapted for most library contests.

The University of Minnesota Libraries include entry tips for the annual student book-collecting contest right on the Web site, as shown in Figure 4-11.

Metropolitan Public Library Name the Bookworm Contest

Tips

1. Follow the rules exactly:

—Fully complete the correct entry form

—Keep entry within established contest limits

—Adhere to age guidelines

2. Timeliness:

—Know when entry is due and where to submit it

—Allow enough time to prepare the entry

—Take into consideration vacation times and other times out of town

—Submit entry ahead of time if you may be away on deadline day

—Try not to wait until the very last minute to submit the entry

—When mailing an entry, be sure to meet the postmark deadline which is prior to the hand delivery deadline

3. Neatness and accuracy:

—Check entry for smudges or tears

—Check for correct grammar and spelling

—Enclose entry in a protective covering if appropriate

—Make sure the entry is not too fragile to be moved easily

—Write legibly (printing or typing is preferred)

4. Creativity:

—Add something to your entry to make it stand out (keeping in mind the entry guidelines, of course)

—Think of all the approaches a person might take to the contest, then try something someone else might not think of

—Put your own personality stamp on the entry

Figure 4-10. Sample Checklist for Contest Entrants

UNIVERSITYLIBRARIES **L U M I N A**
UNIVERSITY OF MINNESOTA

Examples & Tips for a Winning Entry

Examples of annotations from previous winners:

Pastoureau, Michel. 1996. *Figures de l'heraldique*. Paris: Gallimard.
Pastoureau is one of the leading scholars of heraldry, and this is one of his thirty or so books, few of which have been translated into English. This book is copiously illustrated, and serves as both an introduction to the topic and to some of Pastoureau's own original theories.
    From "On Heraldry" by Jonathan Good

Fiffer, Steve. 2000. *Tyrannosaurus Sue: The Extraordinary Saga of the Largest, Most Fought-over T. Rex Ever Found*. New York: W. H. Freeman.
This is an award-winning account of the controversy surrounding the acquisition and rightful ownership of "Sue," the most famous dinosaur specimen in the world. Although this story focuses on the legal battles waged before the specimen was acquired by the Field Museum, this book is especially interesting to me because I worked on the Sue Project for the Field.
    From "My Collection of Books on the History of Vertebrate Paleontology" by Paul Brinkman

Ashley, Mike, ed. *The Mammoth Book of Arthurian Legends*. London: Robinson, 1998.
This collection is a comprehensive introduction to the many facets of Arthurian legend. It includes works by virtual founders of the legends, such as Geoffrey of Monmouth and Alfred, Lord Tennyson, as well as modern writers by Jane Yolen and Phyllis Ann Karr.
    From "My Collection of Arthurian Literature," by Amber B. Shields

Tips:

- TITLE: Give your entry a title to reflect the subject or meaning of the collection.
- COLLECTION COHESION: The strength of a collection derives as much from the collector's knowledge of the subject as from the importance of any particular book or the subject. A miscellaneous group of books that haphazardly make a library held together only by the fact of ownership will not compete successfully against collections that illuminate a topic.
- FORMAT: Collections need not be limited to books, and hardcovers are not necessarily superior to paperbacks. However, most collectors value materials in good condition, and realize that books in poor condition need justification.
- EXPERTISE: The ideal bibliography not only identifies the materials it lists, but also displays the intellectual powers of its compiler. You may arrange the entries in your bibliography in any meaningful way, i.e. alphabetically by author or title, or chronologically, or geographically, if applicable, or by sub-topics. Your bibliography must be annotated. You may follow any annotation and bibliographic style, but follow it consistently.
- PROOF: Proofread your essays and bibliographies, and follow a consistent style. Errors in grammar, spelling, or punctuation tend to distract rather than to persuade readers.

Figure 4-11. Contest Tips Screengrab
(© Regents of the University of Minnesota. All Rights Reserved.)

CONCLUSION

One of your key jobs as the contest planner is to help the staff to help the entrant be challenged and to have fun. A library contest is not homework or a job assignment. As the contest planner, remind all involved it is not just "work." Have a good plan appropriate to your particular contest in place before you begin. Make sure everyone involved is kept up to date on what is going on throughout the project. Set clear eligibility criteria and contest rules. Have an easy-to-understand entry form. Provide a tip sheet if it is appropriate to the type of contest your library is planning. It can help staff remain somewhat free from having to answer the same questions repeatedly, but it might not be necessary for every contest. Ask the staff if a tip sheet or some type of question-and-answer sheet would be helpful. If the answer is yes, help prepare it. This will be another piece of the puzzle for holding a successful library contest.

5 SCHEDULE THE CONTEST

After you have determined the contest's eligibility criteria and rules, the next step is to set the date for your contest and create a schedule from start to finish for the contest.

Choice of contest scheduling is community specific. Only you can know what will work for your community. The biggest factor to consider here is what else is going on in town, at school, or on campus at the time you are considering for your contest. Do not let big events elsewhere deter you from holding a contest at the same time, but do carefully think through whether the event is likely to help or hurt. If you can design your contest to be a part of and run concurrently with a larger community or school event or celebration, you may actually increase participation and interest in the library contest. Large conferences, regional music festivals, sports tournaments, campus events, and community history celebrations can be very compatible with library contests.

In order to schedule your contest, you need to make three decisions first:

1. Will the contest be tied to a specific event?
2. How long will the contest be?
3. Will it be a one-time event or an annual event?

Milestone library or community celebrations such as centennials are times many libraries hold a contest. Grand openings, National Library Week celebrations, naming opportunities, and the introduction of a new service or unique item all are appropriate times to consider holding a library contest. The next section of this chapter discusses each special promotional time that could include a contest. When choosing one of these seven significant times, consider the goals already established by your library.

SEVEN SIGNIFICANT TIMES

TIME 1: MILESTONE CELEBRATIONS

How old or new the library is will determine the milestone you choose to celebrate. Some very old libraries decide to celebrate in a big way only the major milestones—50, 100, 150, and 200 years. The Broward County Library in Ft. Lauderdale, Florida celebrated its 25-year anniversary with the theme "Building on a Tradition of Service." Numerous events, including contests, were held throughout the year to mark the anniversary. Other libraries celebrate every ten or 25 years. Younger libraries sometimes celebrate five-year increments. Some libraries make a milestone of Andrew Carnegie's birthday if they operate from a Carnegie building. One public library chose to celebrate 149 years instead of 150 for its unique public relations value. Some libraries celebrate at the half year if the actual date conflicts with some other community-wide activity. Most milestone celebrations center on the age of library buildings or the date of the library's establishment. Some librarians have chosen to make a milestone out of a service milestone, for instance, the one millionth book added to the collection—the contest centers on when will it happen—or the 100,000th (pick your own number) patron to get a library card. The contest planner can select almost anything to be a milestone and plan a contest around it.

TIP: A contest centered on a library service milestone offers a great value and creates great public relations opportunities.

TIME 2: GRAND OPENINGS

Grand openings of new buildings, new additions, or parts or rooms of the library are "grand" times to hold contests. You can plan the contest around the building materials of the library. For example, guessing the number of bricks, windows, or stones used in the construction of the building are popular contests to generate additional interest in the new library building. When designing such a contest, avoid facts that might have been published when the building was first announced. If there is a unique feature to the building, such as a mosaic, featured art work, or sculpture, that feature can be highlighted. One contest centers around guessing the number of hours it took to create a sculpture, another around how many individual pieces were in the mosaic entry floor.

You can also feature the old building in your contest. Successful essay contests have been held on the theme "My Favorite Memory of the Old Library." Photo contests often are held featuring the old building. These contests are popular if the old library building will be used for a nonlibrary use or is scheduled for demolition. One library took the contest photos of the old building and collected them into a booklet that was a memento given away at the opening of the new library.

TIME 3: NATIONAL LIBRARY CELEBRATIONS

The American Library Association (ALA) has designated several special weeks for which they pick themes and develop materials to be purchased. These focused, celebratory times are tailor-made times to hold a library contest. National Library Week in April, Children's Book Week in November, Banned Books Week and Library Card Sign-Up Month both in September, and Teen Read Week in October are such annual celebrations. Often merchandise developed around these celebrations can be prizes for the contest. Several of the events have a graphics CD associated with the week that you can purchase. On the CD are graphics on the theme that could be localized by the contest planner. Check the ALA Web site, www.ala.org, for the most recent materials, themes, and dates for these national celebratory events.

> **TIP:** National Library Celebrations are great promotion not only for your library but for all libraries.

The Missoula Public Library in Montana selected September, National Library Card Sign-Up Month, as their big contest month. They have made "contest month" an annual event. Their library contests are focused in that one month, and there is something for patrons of all ages, from coloring contests for the youngest children to top ten lists (Top Ten Reasons I Come to the Missoula Public Library) for teens. Area businesses also get on board by offering discounts to people who show their library cards during September.*

TIME 4: DIVERSITY CELEBRATIONS AND FEDERAL HOLIDAYS

Observances such as federal holidays like Martin Luther King Day, President's Day, and the Fourth of July, and designated months such as Black History Month, Women's History Month, and Asian-Pacific Month are all times that could include a contest. Many libraries sponsor essay contests during the Martin Luther King celebrations. The holiday-themed contest ideas are limitless. Figure 5-1 lists some ideas.

> **TIP:** Holidays and other celebrations create great opportunities for essay or poetry contests.

TIME 5: NAMING OPPORTUNITIES

A contest designed around naming something in the library can generate a tremendous amount of interest from your customers and the community in general. For one thing, naming contests are easy to enter, so they have a broad appeal. That simplicity also makes them more appealing to local media outlets, thereby increasing your chances for news coverage of your contest and publicity for your library.

*Missoula Public Library Internet Branch: http://www.missoula.lib.mt.us/signup.html.

HOLIDAY THEME CONTEST IDEAS

Essay or short story contests in which the topic relates directly
to the theme

Online trivia contest

Dress like a historical figure contest

Design a family tree contest

Photography contest focusing on historical markers/statues
in the community

Design a bookmark contest

Themed poster contest

Dress your pet as a past president contest

Design a timeline contest

Figure 5-1. Holiday Theme Contest Ideas

Naming contests come in all shapes and sizes. For example, when a library decides to introduce a mascot, it is a good opportunity to hold a Name the Mascot contest or even a contest to decide what type of animal or object the mascot should be. In 2005, the Arapahoe Library District in Colorado drew 662 entries to its Name-the-Mascot contest (see Figure 5-2). The contest was open to children and teens, from preschool to high school age. "Tales, the Reading Raccoon" emerged as the winning name. Mascots increase attention to your project. Big Cat, the popular mascot at Broward County Library in Florida, is pictured in Figure 5-3.

When a library introduces a new online catalog, it often holds a contest to name the catalog. These contests often have many entries because the entrants know that if their suggested name is selected it will be used for a long time. Many of the winners of Name-the-Catalog contests incorporate "cat" in the winning entry. SunCat, for example, was used in the late 1980s at the Broward County Library in Ft. Lauderdale (see Figure 5-4). Other prize-winning catalog names at other libraries include Zip Cat and Fast Cat. The Lexington Public Library in Kentucky had a contest among staff to name its new browser. The winning entry, Thoro-Browser, and its attendant logo were quickly embraced by the community and staff (see Figure 5-5).

 ARAPAHOE LIBRARY DISTRICT

Home ◄ Programs & Classes ◄ Mascot Contest ◄ Name-the-Mascot Contest ◄

MASCOT
CONTEST

Print friendly version

Updated 07/01/2005

The Official 2005 Name-the-Mascot Contest

for Children and Teens — Preschool - Grade 12

Our New Mascot Has a Name!

Judges for the Name-the-Mascot Contest looked over 662 wonderful entries from young people of all ages from all of our libraries. The creativity of those who entered is amazing but, in the end, the judges had the difficult job of choosing only one.

The name selected for the new Arapahoe Library District mascot is . . . **Tales, the Reading Raccoon**.

Three young people (ages 9-10) from the Glendale, Koelbel and Smoky Hill libraries submitted the winning name, and each one will receive a prize. We're also making plans to honor six runners-up (ages 4-11) from the Koelbel, Sheridan, Smoky Hill and Southglenn libraries with a small prize because they came close to the selected name - with their entries of Big Tail, Black & White Tale, and Ring Tale or Ring Tail. We'll be contacting the winners and the runners-up by phone soon to arrange for them to pick up their prizes.

Thanks to everyone who entered the contest, and watch for **Tales, the Reading Raccoon** soon at your library.

Tales, the Reading Raccoon is funded by the Friends of the Arapahoe Library District. Many thanks for their continued support of library programs and services.

Home | Search this Site | Contact Us | Electronic Resources / Internet Policy

Find Books, Videos, CDs...
Renew & Request Items
Library Card/Account

Research & Reference
Readers Corner
Videos, DVDs, etc.
Programs & Classes
About Us
More Library Resources

Search this Site
Search the Web
Contact Us
Text Only

Trip to Ireland
Getting More

Special Events
Coat Drive
Kids Programs
Ask Colorado
Homework Help
Holiday Programs
Research Databases
Job Resources
Email Newsletter
Teen Newsletter

**Figure 5-2. Name-the-Mascot Contest
(Reproduced by permission of the Arapahoe Library District.)**

Figure 5-3. Mascots increase attention to your project. Pictured here is Big Cat, popular mascot at Broward County Library in Florida.

Figure 5-4. The Sun Cat was a popular figure at the Broward County Library in Florida.

Figure 5-5. ThoroBrowser reflects the character of the community in Central Kentucky's Bluegrass Region, where Lexington is designated "the Horse Capital of the World."

TIME 6: LIBRARY DESIGNATED TIMES

The contest planner can choose any time to hold a contest. Some libraries choose to hold their contests each year during one particular month or week. When states hold contests to select the best children's books of the year, they have the contest at the same time each year and have their prize winner announcement at the same time each year. Washington, Florida, South Carolina, and Kentucky are among the many states that hold annual statewide Best Book contests.

Your library should decide if it wants to hold contests regularly—annually, monthly, or seasonally—or just occasionally. You need to evaluate your local situation to determine what will be most successful.

TIME 7: INTRODUCTION OF NEW OR UNIQUE SERVICES

Libraries often tie the publicity for a new or unique service to a contest. When many libraries introduce new looks to their Web pages, they hold a Web contest to get people to the newly designed site.

Some libraries have contests themed around "How Using the Library Helped Me" or "How the New Grants Collection Helped Me," for example. Again, the opportunities to design a contest around a new or unique service are almost limitless.

CONTEST LENGTH

Another important decision in scheduling your library contest is the length. The contest length is the period of time between the announcement of the contest and the announcement of the winners. Within that period you must determine when you will begin accepting entries and when the entry deadline is. If the contest is for a work of art, the period the contest is open would be longer to allow prospective entrants to create the work. Photo contests, essay contests, and art for display contests usually have longer contest periods—typically two months between open and close. Sometimes you keep a contest open longer so you can promote it longer. Some contests are open only for the week they are celebrating. Some contests have a very short length. The contest length may be only the length of the event itself, like a contest held during a grand opening event. Consider if the time allowed between opening and closing of the contest is truly adequate to receive the maximum number of entries. Holding the contest during busy times of the year, holidays, back to

TIP: Check your local community calendar, often compiled by the Chamber of Commerce, before selecting contest dates.

TIP: Successful contests are just long enough.

school, or community-wide celebrations may limit the amount of participation unless the contest is directly tied to the event and has an adequate open time.

The Houston Public Library held an Easter Egg hunt that lasted an hour during Easter week. The twist was that the hunt was targeted at teens. They won prizes for collecting the most eggs. The success lay in that there was a clear holiday tie-in, the contest was extremely limited in time scope, it had a narrow age focus to go along with the limited time, and it was held on a Thursday before the busy Easter weekend. Make sure there are no similar or competing activities going on in your community when you choose your contest dates.

The time required for judging is important to decide before you prepare your contest schedule. Some contests, such as a guessing contest, require only a day to review the entries to find the winner. Other contests, such as essay or poster contests, may take several weeks to judge and select the winners. The contest planner or team will need to estimate the number of entries that might be submitted and also think about how long it will take for the contest judges to do their work. If the library has held contests previously, check how these factors were determined previously. If the library is planning its first contest, check with other community organizations to find out information about contest participation.

When you determine the length of the contest, remember to have it long enough so that people have adequate time to enter. Potential contest entrants need time to have heard about the contest, time to weigh whether or not to enter, and time to prepare and submit their entry. It is critical to know your community so you can adequately judge these times for your community.

Sometimes contests have an open time of months. While this does give the public plenty of time to prepare their entry and also gives the library plenty of time to promote the contest, the long open contest time can be detrimental to the contest's success. People can lose interest or even forget about entering. The best contest has just the right amount of open time. Make sure to avoid holidays or weekends for contest closing dates. Most contests close at 5 P.M. on a Friday. Talk with other staff or community event planners and solicit their comments on your proposed contest length.

ONE-TIME CONTESTS VERSUS RECURRING CONTESTS

Another scheduling factor is whether or not your contest will be a one-time event or a regularly occurring one. There are advantages to both. If the contest is planned annually around a special event or time, people learn to anticipate it. An annual contest requires less publicity as the years go on because people know it will be held at a certain time. Annual contests tend to have continued increase in the number of entries. However, if a contest is a one-off, it can have very high interest and many entrants. The decision about annual or one-time depends on your community. Contests that are centered on a milestone, grand opening, or introduction of a new service would all be one-time contests. National Library Week or Children's Book Week contests are good choices for annual contests.

Even though you have decided to hold a contest annually at the same time, the actual contest could vary. For example, if you decide always to hold a contest during Children's Book Week, you could choose to have a children's bookmark design contest as part of each year's celebration, or you could have a photo contest one year, a guessing contest the next year, and a bookmark design contest the third year. Sometimes you hold a contest and plan it as a one-time event, but after it was held and it exceeded your expectations, after the tremendous success, then the contest planner or team recommends that the contest become an annual event.

> **TIP:** Annual contests build anticipation in your community.

PREPARING THE CONTEST SCHEDULE

After you have decided the length of the contest and when the contest will be held, then you are ready to prepare the contest schedule. Items that need to be included in the schedule are as follows:

- Contest time frame and length
- Contest announcement
- Publicity kick-off
- Entry form preparation and distribution
- Contest start
- Entry collection
- Entry deadline
- Collection of entries and delivery to the judging place
- Time to verify eligibility
- Judging
- Preparation of a display of entries, if applicable
- Announcement of winners
- Publicity of winners
- Recognition event, if applicable

- Prize pick-up
- Contest evaluation

CONCLUSION

Effective scheduling of the library contest can make the difference between a contest that is moderately successful and a contest that exceeds expectations. When to hold a contest, how to schedule it, and what event to tie it to are limited only by your staff's creativity. Involve your staff, Friends, volunteers, students, faculty, and library customers in formulating contest ideas. Remember to review your library and contest goals before you decide to schedule your contest. You can even have a contest to come up with the most creative, most original, funniest, or best-themed contests for the upcoming year to help meet your public relations goals. Remember, people like contests because they are fun. Have fun designing your contest, too.

6 SELECT THE PRIZE

By the time you and your team get to the point of selecting the prizes, you are on the home stretch. Choosing the prizes for your contest is really the fun part of the planning process. What will entice people to enter your contest? What would you like to win if you were entering a contest?

The fundamental decision about the prize is whether it will be a tangible merchandise prize or a form of recognition. Different types of contests more closely match different types of prizes. Also, it is important to match the type of audience to the type of prize. The better the match between the prize and the type of audience, the higher the success rate of the contest.

TYPES OF PRIZES

The one element that truly serves to differentiate contests from other types of library programs is the prizes. Everyone likes to win, and the desire to win is most often what inspires people to take the time to enter a contest. As you are planning your own library contest, determining what prizes and how many to award will be a major consideration. Prizes given in library contests fall into eleven major areas:

1. General Merchandise
2. Library-Related Merchandise
3. Celebrity or Author Items or Merchandise
4. Recognition Items
5. Name in Print, On-Air, or Exhibit Prizes
6. Trips
7. Food and Drink
8. Monetary Prizes
9. Clothing Items
10. Attraction or Event Tickets and Passes
11. Other Unique Prizes

Each of these categories will be treated in detail in this chapter. As part of the planning process, consideration must be given to what type of prize or reward will be given. Let us take a closer look at factors to consider when determining what prizes you want to offer with your contest.

THE NUMBER AND LEVELS OF PRIZES

TIP: For contestants, the prize is often the most important aspect of the contest, so choose prizes wisely.

How many prizes will you give in the contest? Some contests give a prize to every entrant or register every entrant for the grand prize drawing. Summer reading programs typically give a prize to every finisher. If you give a prize of some kind to every participant, will there be enough enthusiasm for the contest? Also, if you give a small prize to everyone, will the participants consider the prize cheap or not worth their while to enter? These are the types of questions contest planners must consider when choosing prizes. You will lose goodwill if many contest participants are dissatisfied with the prize. You need to carefully consider the merits of only giving selected prizes versus giving one to everybody. If you do choose the option of one prize for all, make sure the prize is age appropriate.

Sometimes the nature of the contest itself determines the number of winners possible. For instance, if the contest is to design the cover of the library's annual report, that would necessarily limit the winner to only one. Other examples of when you might have only a limited number of winners include the following: (1) an essay contest with themes like "Why I Want to Be a Librarian for a Day" or "Why I Would Like to Meet Richard Peck"; (2) a playwriting contest where the prize is a performance of the winning entry by the local children's theater; and (3) the American Library Association (ALA)'s Major Leagues@your library, where the grand prize was a trip for two to the World Series.

TIP: Seeking a donated prize from the community can create great partnership opportunities with area businesses and organizations. Make sure to clearly recognize and thank the business that donated the prize in your contest publicity.

If you decide to give a limited number of prizes, your selection will depend on several factors. Do you have money in the budget to buy prizes? Do you anticipate having the prizes donated or provided by the Friends of the Library? Do you plan to use items the library already has in stock, such as library t-shirts or library tote bags? Will some form of recognition be the prize so there will be no direct costs? Will you work with a partner to provide a service as some other type of prize?

Review the advantages and disadvantages of having a tiered system of prizes, for example, first, second, third, or grand prize and runners-up for your particular contest. If you use a tiered system of prize awards, you will need to have judges qualified to review and pick the best and then further refine to reach a scaled selection of winners. The more levels of prizes, the longer the process of judging will take. Also, it will increase the possibility of discussion and lack of satisfaction with the selection of the winners. In small, rural towns, sometimes it is difficult to find enough people qualified on a certain topic who are available for contest judging on the library's time schedule. Keeping the levels of prizes to the base number to meet the contest goals will increase your chances of success. Some contests are also designed with a set number of equal winners.

In school reading contests, often children will review the list of available awards at the start of the contest and decide which prizes they want. They will then complete the prize points necessary to obtain the items selected. This computation serves as the child's personal goal and is often higher than a goal set by a teacher or librarian. When the contest takes place over several weeks or a school semester, there is the question of determining when the prizes should be awarded. The children should be able to complete their points easily at any given time. Some of the impact may be lost by not giving out the awards as each level of achievement is reached and giving them out at an end-of-the-semester assembly. State clearly in the contest rules when children can receive their awards.

In a longer contest, certificates could be given out to provide interim recognition. Periodic issuing of point recognition certificates also can help head off misunderstandings before they occur.

When the contest is a scaled level of accomplishment contest, it is not recommended to include a high value prize that no one could hope to win. A grand prize does stimulate additional interest, and the contestant not only competes with himself or herself but also seeks the additional recognition as the outstanding performer.

Your contest might be divided by age categories. There might be a prize or prizes for children and a prize or prizes for adults, or some other age breakdown. The type of prize should match your contest eligibility criteria. Other categories to consider for some contests would be amateur and professional. If you have a photography contest, you might have different types of prizes for new photographers and the seasoned professional photographers. Prizes in the same contest might also vary by grade level in school.

> **TIP:** A tiered award system is a good choice for a contest with many entries. It can make the judges' job easier because it is often difficult to choose a single winner from a group of superior finishers.

> **TIP:** Make sure the prize is appropriate for the contest entrant's age and interest level.

ATTRACTIVENESS, APPEAL, AND APPROPRIATENESS OF PRIZE

When selecting the prize for the contest, consider if the prize will engender enough participation to make the contest worthwhile. Even the smallest, most simple contest takes planning, staff time, publicity, and judging or awarding. You want to have adequate participation. Ask a few nonlibrary friends if they think the prize would entice them to enter the contest and

TIP: If the contest is for all ages, the prize should be usable regardless of age.

TIP: A good rule of thumb is the more general the contest audience, the more general the prize.

TIP: Take care to match the prize to the contest.

consider their feedback before making the final selection. If you design a contest for all ages, will the prize be appealing to all age groups? Food, money, and recognition are prizes that transcend all age groups. A pogo stick would be a poor choice in this case; movie passes would be better. A DVD is not an attractive prize for people without a DVD player. The more uniform the appeal of the prize, the greater the contest participation.

If free coupons, gift certificates, or free admissions are your prizes, are the locations of the stores, restaurants, sporting venues, and attractions within a reasonable distance from the service area of the library? Many statewide summer reading programs award discount passes to attractions within their state to all summer program finishers. How motivating is it for an inner-city child to receive discount tickets to a baseball park that is not accessible by public transportation and has a $10 parking fee or to receive a 10 percent off coupon for a $56 theme pass ticket to a park four hours away?

Is the prize you are considering so unusual that many people either could not use it or would not want it? Some mediocre art work would fall into this category. Some libraries have contests to give away the progeny of the library gerbils, rats, snakes, or guinea pigs. Not all parents allow their children to have pets. There might be allergy problems for the child who wins the animal and then great disappointment when the child cannot keep the pet. Pets do not make appropriate contest prizes—unless they are stuffed animals!

Trips that contain some but not all of the costs also are not recommended. Sometimes library staff can get airfare or hotel rooms donated but not both. In this situation, it would be wise to look for another prize, because a trip that is only half funded limits the number of people who could truly benefit from the trip and would not be an incentive for many potential entrants.

Is the prize motivational to get the target audience to take the action you had set as the contest's goal? Often schools, colleges, and universities give prizes to students on their first visit to the library after completing a library quiz. A key thought to keep in mind when choosing prizes for your contest is in most cases, people enter the contest because of the prize. The prize is the motivation.

THE VALUE OF THE LIBRARY LOGO

The next factor to consider when selecting the prize is whether or not the prize itself will be an advertising mechanism and contain the library's logo. The categories of prizes such as food and drink, trips, monetary items, and some tangible but non-library-related gifts will come without your logo or recognition. In these situations, try to have stickers with the library name and logo that can be affixed to these items. For a recent summer reading program, the Lexington Public Library in Kentucky used inexpensively produced Summer Reader stickers with the library's name on them to affix to summer reading contest items (see Figure 6-1). Trip tickets can be packaged in library-logoed envelopes. Have the cash prizes be library checks in library envelopes. Logos can also be affixed to the prize boxes.

Figure 6-1. Summer Reader Sticker
(Reproduced by permission of the Lexington Public Library.)

The way to meet two contest objectives—public relations for the library and continued message recognition—is to have the prize be a library-logoed item. That way, every time the winner wears or uses the prize, the library's logo is on display. Clothing, library-related tangible items such as backpacks, water bottles, and mugs and regular library promotional items such as pencils, bookmarks, and stickers are all examples of library-logoed items that make successful prizes (see Figure 6-2).

Figure 6-2. Imprinted Logo Items

If the prize is an event, try to make sure that the event is at the library or that there is at least plenty of recognition of the library as the contest sponsor.

Staff in some libraries feel that all library contests need to have a library-specific prize. Later on in this chapter is a list of sample library-specific and library-themed prizes for you to review. Some examples would be t-shirts with the library's logo on them, key chains with the library's logo on them, or library logo-printed lanyards.

Others think that a non-library-specific prize is more of an incentive to the people in their area. The other option is to give winners library-related items such as bookends, book character stuffed animals, and autographed books.

PRIZES AS PUBLIC RELATIONS

If you were to give away a candy bar to all winners of a Guess the Number of Hershey's Kisses in the Jar on the Circulation Desk contest, for instance, you might have happy, candy-loving winners, but there would be little news value to it. However, if you have a lunch with J.K. Rowling for the winner of the Why I Want to Meet the Author of the Harry Potter Books Essay Contest, it would be a huge media event. Whether this factor, the public relations or news value of the prize, was one of your goals or not will determine how much weight you give to this factor. If your goal was to bring 5 percent more children in a certain age group into the library during a month and the Guess the Number of Candies in a Jar contest did that, this factor is not as important. A win-win situation can be if your prize selection encourages people to participate in the target activity and garners some additional publicity for the library.

AUTHORS AND OTHER CELEBRITIES

You need to decide if the use of a celebrity-related prize will fit into your contest. There are many different celebrity prizes you can consider. Signed items are one idea. These include autographed books, pictures, or an item owned by the celebrity. The prize could be the opportunity to meet the author or celebrity, to spend some time at his or her place of work, to have a meal with the person, or even to have a picture taken with the celebrity.

When determining what celebrity to use, consider first if everyone will recognize the name of the celebrity. If many potential contestants do not, the use of a celebrity will not be helpful. Consider carefully if the celebrity is someone with whom you want the library's name associated. One library used dinner with a well-known but outspoken athlete who was a hometown boy as the prize for a children's program. The library received very negative publicity because some parents did not consider the athlete an admirable person.

Before selecting a celebrity event for a prize, check with several nonlibrary people to get their reaction. The person selected needs to have a broad appeal to be a good selection for a prize. Many celebrities have very tight schedules and sometimes have to cancel on short notice or arrive late. Check with others who have worked with the person you are considering to see how successful their program was. Some local high profile people will be as much of a draw for your contest as out-of-town people with higher celebrity status. Consider local TV personalities, local officials, or local artists and authors.

NAMING PRIZES

If the library is starting a new service, acquiring a library pet, or introducing a new online catalog, it is often advantageous to hold a naming contest in conjunction with the introduction of the new addition to the public. In these types of contests, the prize is that the winner's suggested name is selected and used for the new item or service.

SATISFACTION OF WINNERS AND PARTICIPANTS

TIP: Pick prizes that will make people happy.

Along with meeting the contest goals and objectives, the participants need to feel that the prize was achievable. The winners need to feel that they received the prize that they expected. Describe your contest prize clearly to avoid confusion. It is particularly important with recognition prize contests that there are no misunderstandings of all aspects of the prize. The same is true for trips. If you have different prizes for different ages, another way to achieve winner satisfaction is to announce and repeat these differences. A regular library user mom-to-be was irritated to be refused a stuffed animal prize for reading to her child in vitro, since she had read aloud the required number of children's books. Review the satisfaction of your previous library contest winners. Is there anything you can do to improve upon that?

AVOIDING POTENTIAL PROBLEMS: PEANUTS, GERBILS, AND MANGOES

It is best to try to think of any potential problems there might be with your prize. Some prizes to avoid include foods that are common allergy foods, like peanuts and mangoes, for example; nonfiction books that are one-sided "issue" books; books with poor reviews or in shabby condition; an expensive donated prize with very limited appeal; a very cheap prize that participants would not consider worthy of their effort; antiques of interest only to a limited number of collectors; tickets, gift certificates, or passes to out-of-area or out-of-state attractions; prizes with no obvious connection to the contest; and animals. The better the prize selection for the specific contest, the higher the level of participation you can expect.

THE ROLE OF THE CONTEST PLANNER

The contest planner plays a very important part in the selection of prizes. As the planner, you need to review past contests. The personal likes and dislikes of the contest planner may have a subtle influence on the choice of prizes. If the contest planner does not feel confident enough selecting the prizes, he or she could have a committee choose or ask other library staff to help decide what would fit the community. It is important to be realistic about prize possibilities and numbers rather than to disappoint participants if you are not able at the last minute to come through with the prizes. If the library always does the same contest each year with the same prizes, the contest planner might stretch a little and experiment with some other prizes.

Also keep in mind the value of involving area businesses and organizations in the contest by asking for the donation of a prize. Often businesses like this type of community involvement because it is good public relations. The donated prizes themselves can actually advertise the product or service in which the business sponsor specializes. A good example of this is a writing contest for which the prize is publication of the winning piece in a local magazine or newspaper. A local bookstore might be willing to donate children's books as prizes for a school poster contest. Getting businesses or organizations to donate prizes is usually straightforward. Most companies already have a procedure in place for those requesting donations, so a quick phone call can alert you to those procedures if they exist. If the receptionist does not know if such a procedure exists, ask to speak to someone in the marketing or public relations office. A request letter on your library's letterhead is usually all you will need. Remember to keep your letter clear and specific. Also, if possible, address the letter to a specific person. A "To Whom It May Concern" type of letter will most likely get lost in the shuffle. Figure 6-3 is a sample prize solicitation letter you can adapt to your library contests' specific needs.

Use the handy checklist shown in Figure 6-4 to help determine the best prize for your contest. If you have answered "No" to more than half of these questions, you should rethink your prize selection.

Dear Mrs. Smith:

The (NAME OF LIBRARY) is holding a (NAME OF CONTEST) to (BRIEF DESCRIPTION OF CONTEST GOAL).

We want your company to be a part of the project. The library appreciates the important role you play in the community and knows that your participation will help the contest be a success. The contest planners have identified what they consider to be the best incentives for contest participants. If you could provide (ASK SPECIFICALLY FOR WHAT YOU WANT—TEN T-SHIRTS, 6 PLANTS, TEN CDs, 25 BOOKS), we would greatly appreciate it. These prizes would be given on (DATE OF AWARDS CEREMONY) to the winner or winners at the end of the contest.

We would be happy to have you or a representative of your company come to the awards ceremony and present the prizes. Your company will be listed as the sponsor of the prizes in all the contest publicity. You will also be recognized at the awards ceremony.

If you have any questions, please call (NAME OF LIBRARY CONTACT) at (PHONE NUMBER). I appreciate your consideration of this request. Please let us hear from you by (SPECIFIC DATE). Thank you.

Sincerely,

Figure 6-3. Sample Letter for Soliciting Prizes

Prize Selection Checklist	YES	NO
1. Will the prize engender enough participation to meet the contest objectives?		
2. Is the prize attractive enough to the target audience that they will enter the contest?		
3. Do the people in the target group for your contest value recognition over tangible items?		
4. Do the people in the target group value tangible items over reward?		
5. Will you get extra publicity value from your selected prize?		
6. Is the prize age-appropriate?		
7. If your contest is for all age groups, will the prize/reward be appealing to all age groups?		
8. If coupons or gift certificates are being offered, are the locations of the attractions or restaurants within a reasonable distance from the service area of the library?		
9. Have you done a reality-check with some people outside of the library family to make sure the prize is attractive?		
10. Does the prize/reward match the contest?		
11. If using autographed items, will everyone recognize the celebrity?		
12. Will the autographing celebrity come and make the award in person?		
13. Is the celebrity one you want associated with the library's name?		
14. Have other agencies in your area used the prize?		
15. If giving a small prize to everyone who enters, will the participants consider the prize "cheap"?		
16. Is the prize so unique that many people couldn't use it?		
17. Does the prize require the winner to own some equipment in order to use the prize?		
18. If the answer to #18 is YES, do a large share of the potential contest participants own the required equipment?		
19. Should at least one of the prizes include the equipment?		
20. Can you afford the prize or have it donated?		

Figure 6-4. Prize Selection Checklist

TIP: Carefully consider the type of prize most suited to your community. Observe the types of prizes and incentives other area contests offer and keep your prizes in line.

ELEVEN PRIZE CATEGORIES

The next section of this chapter will review the types of prizes, evaluate the pros and cons of each type, and discuss which types of prizes best match which types of contests.

GENERAL MERCHANDISE

Description: Concrete items such as a mug, CD player, PDA, computer, stuffed animal, plant, handcrafted item, art work, city or regional product, portable music player, water bottle, holiday item, toy, game, baby safety electric plug cover, or knapsack.

Advantages: These items are a direct reward. When a person wins, he or she gets the prize. There is a wide variety of products available. There is a wide range of prices of items. It is easy to find products that match the theme of the contest. The products are fairly easy to get donated. Merchandise prizes are a form of recognition that provides a more permanent reminder that something has been accomplished.

Disadvantages: No link to library because no logo or relationship to library.

Recommended for the following types of contests: General contests, teen contests, contests that match the theme of the product, for example, a stuffed animal for a Name the Mascot contest.

Sample Merchandise Items

- Mugs
- CD players
- DVD players
- TVs
- PDAs
- Computers
- Stuffed animals
- Plants
- Craft or hobby supplies
- Handcrafted items
- Art work
- Portable music players
- Water bottles
- Lunch boxes or bags
- CD or DVD holders
- Holiday items
- Backpacks
- Baby safety electrical outlet covers
- Toys and games
- Bikes
- Computer games

• City or region's local
products

• Flashlights or tools

LIBRARY-RELATED MERCHANDISE

Description: Includes library-logoed items such as stickers,
pins, paper bookmarks, books, CDs, DVDs, graphic novels,
board books, buttons, posters, book-themed articles, tote
bags, pencils, pens, bookends, stationery, engraved or leather
bookmarks, library figurines, lanyards, travel mugs, key
chains, and library card holders. The canvas bag shown in
Figure 6-5 was designed for the 2000 New Hampshire State
Library Summer Reading program.

Advantages: Items are available at time of award, advertise
the library whenever the winner uses the item, advertise
the library to others when they see the winner using the

**Figure 6-5. New Hampshire Book Bag
(Used by permission of the artist, Chris Demarest.)**

prizes, extend goodwill about the library. They are constant reminders of doing something exceptional.

Disadvantages: May or may not be unique to contest winner. The same items might be available for sale to all or as giveaways for other library-related programs.

Recommended for the following types of contests: General contests, author-related contests, writing and essay contests, contests with many entrants, contests in which the primary goal is to raise the library awareness, contests in which the prize matches the contest theme.

Sample Library-Related Prizes

- Books
- CDs
- DVDs
- Graphic novels
- Board books
- Stickers
- Pins
- Buttons
- Posters
- Book theme items, for example, stuffed Clifford the Dog
- Lanyards
- Bookmarks
- Candy jars
- Stadium cushions
- Calculators
- Tote bags
- Pencils or pens
- Bookends
- Stationery
- Leather or engraved bookmarks
- Figurines
- Framed book illustrations
- Key chains
- Library card holders
- Individualized READ posters
- Travel mugs
- Clocks
- Paperweights
- Wristbands
- Magnets

CELEBRITY OR AUTHOR ITEMS OR MERCHANDISE

Description: Includes items such as autographed books, a picture of a celebrity, a picture with a celebrity, a meal with the author, meeting a celebrity/author, visiting the celebrity at his or her place of work, a visit to a politician's office, or an autographed item from a celebrity.

Advantages: Items do not cost the library anything if the celebrity is local, people like personalized items and autographed items, and autographed items are highly collectible.

Disadvantages: If the individual does not like the celebrity or author, that person probably will not participate; the celebrity might lack the name recognition necessary to promote the contest effectively or to motivate participation; the library may only be able to have one celebrity or author prize; and the featured person might be late or cancel altogether.

Recommended for the following types of contests: Contests in which you need a lot of media attention and high participation, contests aimed at the age group with which the celebrity or author is most popular, contests centered around the author's book(s), themed contests centered around the topic of the celebrity's fame, contests in which you have a large enough venue to hold recognition events, and writing, poetry, or art contests.

Sample Celebrity or Author Prizes

- Autographed books
- Picture with a celebrity
- Meal with an author
- Meet a celebrity
- Get something autographed by a celebrity
- Visit a celebrity at his or her place of work
- Visit to a politician's office, for example, meet the mayor or the senator

RECOGNITION ITEMS

Description: Recognition on TV or radio, featured spot in a parade, featured recognition at a community event, newspaper article, picture, or feature, framed photo of recognition event, being featured on local TV, and being featured in national media. Some recognition contests do include a certificate, medal, ribbon, or ceremony as a tangible part of the recognition. Certificates are inexpensive recognition items that you can easily make yourself on the computer. Print them on fancy paper and put them in a certificate frame from the dollar store, and you have a great award for your winners (see Figure 6-6).

Recognition contests attract different people than do tangible award contests. Talk to your staff, Friends of the Library, and others to get their ideas on which type of prize will attract the most participants in your area. Contests that involve creative efforts, art, photography, and writing often have recognition as the prize. Having a contest to select art to hang in the library for a short time or perma-

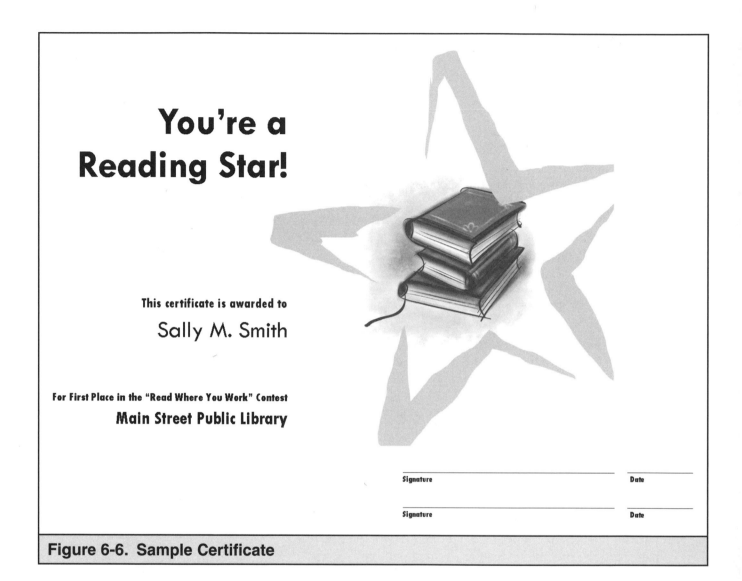

Figure 6-6. Sample Certificate

TIP: Recognition prizes cost little and have great public relations value.

nently or art to use in library publications are popular and low cost. How many creative people live in your community? Can your contest help to spur creativity? Richard Florida's book *The Rise of the Creative Class* will help you learn more about your community and creativity. Check with photography clubs, writing workshops, and local playwrights to gather information about interest in a recognition prize for creative efforts. A writing contest can help encourage young writers and give them a venue for their work.

Other types of recognition can also be the prize. Examples include a featured spot in a parade or other important community event, or a chance to be featured on local or national TV or radio. The grand prize winner of the Major

Leagues @ Your Library contest was on national TV. The local or regional newspapers and magazines often give additional recognition to the contest winner.

Advantages: Great opportunities for library recognition in media, challenges people's creativity, good match with goals, low cost, and strengthens community partnerships.

Disadvantages: High amount of time necessary for judging, and necessary to have specialized judges.

Recommended for the following types of contests: Writing contest, art contest, poster and bookmark design contest, and photograph contest.

Sample Recognition Prizes

- Recognition on TV or radio through news or public service announcements
- Part of an awards ceremony
- Trophy
- Plaque
- Ribbon
- Certificate
- Chance to be featured on a local TV program
- Medal or other commemorative piece
- Featured spot in a parade or other local event
- Framed photo of recognition event
- Framed newspaper article about winner

NAME IN PRINT, ON-AIR, OR EXHIBIT PRIZES

Description: All art work exhibited, art work used for official library publication or annual report, writing or photography featured in national media, name in print, work published, work performed, work exhibited, work purchased by or permanently hung in library.

Advantages: Winner satisfaction, low cost, provides library with quality art, strengthens community partnerships.

Disadvantages: Amount of time necessary for judging, locating qualified judges, amount of space needed for exhibit.

Recommended for the following types of contests: Writing contest, art contest, playwriting contest, photography contest, essay or poetry contest, and book-related contest.

Sample Name in Print, On-Air, or Exhibit Prizes

- Name in print
- Work exhibited
- Work published
- Work performed
- Art work used for official library promotion

- Art work included in library annual report
- Writing or photography featured in a national magazine
- All art work exhibited

TRIPS

Description: Trip to specific locations, trip to a place connected to the contest, trip on special local transportation (like a steam railway, hot air balloon, canal boat), trip to a literary landmark, or trip to meet an author.

Advantages: Can be very contest specific, for example, Why I Want to Visit Faulkner's Birthplace or Why I Want to Meet Lemony Snicket; if for children or teens, expands their horizons, popular with entrants, increases number of contest participants. Although a trip prize does not have the tangible permanency of merchandise, many potential contest entrants consider trips far superior to either cash or merchandise prizes. An all-expense-paid trip is an award that will be long remembered, and the digital photos can be shared with many at home and provide tangible, long-lasting reminders of the trip in future years.

Disadvantages: Details can be time consuming; if a trip has to be taken at a specific time only, it could be a problem if the winner could not go then; there is usually a big difference between first prize (the trip) and other prizes; people might not be attracted to travel to the specific location of the trip; and bad weather might delay or cancel the trip.

Recommended for the following types of contests: Contests with travel themes, contests that need high motivation to enter.

Sample Trip Prizes

- Trip to a place connected to the contest

- Trip to a conference
- Trip to a national contest

- Trip on special local transportation, for example, a canal boat, steam railway, or hot air balloon
- Trip to a literary landmark
- Trip to meet an author
- Trip to another library
- Trip with a corporate sponsor (for example, by company jet or on the bus with a baseball team)

FOOD AND DRINK

Description: food event for all participants, restaurant meals, food for individual winner and guest, candy, condiments, gourmet food, fruit or specialty food in gift baskets, wine.

Advantages: popular because people like to eat; food parties as a prize for all entrants attract high participation.

Disadvantages: food allergies, people might not like or be able to eat the food prize, constant food prizes might reinforce the idea of using food for reward, potential problem to nondrinkers if prize is wine or alcohol.

Recommended for the following types of contests: Low-cost contests, food-related contests.

Sample Food and Drink Prizes

- Restaurant meals
- Candy and condiments
- Gourmet food
- Locally made wine
- Food event for a group—ice cream or pizza party
- Fruit or specialty food item baskets
- Chocolate
- Cookbooks
- Regional food specialty items

MONETARY PRIZES

Description: Savings bond, cash, gift certificates or gift cards

Advantages: Very popular, can be used for all age groups and with people of all interests. Cash is one of the older forms of prizes. The fact that monetary awards have a long history as prizes is evidence that they are contestant pleasing. Money, gift certificates, gift cards, and savings bonds are popular with all ages. Extra money is always welcome and provides impetus for entering the contest.

Disadvantages: Some people do not understand that a savings bond is not the same as immediate cash; some people think it is not an appropriate award for creative contests; gift certificates and gift cards are not immediate rewards, must be used at a later date, must be obtained from Friends or donors as most libraries cannot give away library funds; sometimes the amount of cash is considered too small to be an incentive.

Recommended for the following types of contests: Can be used for almost any type of contest.

Sample Monetary Prizes

- Savings bonds
- Cash
- Gift certificates
- Coupons
- Scholarships
- Gift cards

CLOTHING ITEMS

Description: T-shirt, hat, bib, sweatshirt, polo shirt, tie—all with library logo.

Advantages: Popular with winners, provide free advertising for the library.

Disadvantages: Items are not unique, might be obtainable from other places and so do not provide much motivation for entrants.

Recommended for the following types of contests: Can be used for almost any contest.

Sample Clothing Prizes

- T-shirts
- Bibs
- Sweatshirts
- Polo shirts
- Ties
- Ball caps
- Jackets
- Jewelry

ATTRACTION OR EVENT TICKETS AND PASSES

Description: Movie passes, local attraction tickets, sporting event tickets, museum passes, zoo and aquarium passes, concert tickets, and tickets to literary events.

Advantages: Low cost because they are usually donated by the partnership organization, popular with young people.

Disadvantages: Low interest level if the person has no transportation or poor public transportation so people cannot use them; some have a short life and expire shortly after being awarded.

Recommended for the following types of contests: Summer reading programs, children's and youth programs, theme contests that match the attraction theme.

Sample Attraction or Event Tickets or Passes Prizes

- Movie passes
- Local attraction tickets
- Sporting event tickets
- Museum passes
- Zoo or aquarium passes
- Tickets to literary events
- Theatre or symphony tickets
- Concert tickets

OTHER UNIQUE PRIZES

Description: Opportunity to do something special, be the first at something, use a new service for the first time, be a librarian for a day, discounts, tickets to a preview of a library special event, commemorative items for special library events, or winner's name in a famous author's next book (see Figure 6-7).

Picture with a celebrity or sports star	Name in a famous author's next book
Visit a celebrity at his or her place of work	Visit to a politician's office and meet the mayor or senator, for instance
Meet a celebrity	
Get something autographed by a celebrity	Featured spot in a parade or other local event
Get your name in print	Ticket to preview library events
Have your work exhibited	Chance to be featured on a local TV program
Opportunity to do something first, like trying out a new library service	Writing or art work featured in a national magazine
Be a librarian for a day	Art work included in library annual report
Be part of an awards ceremony	
Recognition on TV or radio	

Figure 6-7. Sample Prizes That Cost Nothing but Time

Advantages: Something unique attracts a large number of participants, creates excitement, low cost.

Disadvantages: Depending on the choice of activity, could attract a limited number of entrants.

Recommended for the following types of contests: Contests with unique goals, contests trying to reach new audiences.

Sample Other Prizes

- Opportunity to do something special (first in new service, first through the door of the new library branch)
- Be a librarian for a day
- Discounts

- Ticket to preview library events
- Name in famous author's book (having a character named for you)

CONCLUSION

Keep in mind that combinations of prizes might also be given. A small merchandise prize may be given to all contestants who enter (see Figures 6-8 and 6-9). In addition, a trip or cash award might be given to the top three winners.

The type of prize selected must be consistent with the goals of the contest. Sufficient incentive always must be offered to encourage full and enthusiastic participation. It is naive to assume that a contestant would be stimulated to enter a library contest that would take many hours to craft or develop the entry for if the contestant received only a photocopied certificate indicating that he or she was the winner. However, if well-developed, quality plaques or trophies are the prize, they provide a permanent record of the accomplishment, and people take pride in displaying their award. If the staff recognition award is strategically placed in the library, it also can serve as a constant reminder to all staff that achievers are recognized. Careful selection of the right prizes for the contest goes a long way toward ensuring a high level of participation in the contest as well as satisfied participants and winners and a public relations success.

As you can see, you need to make many decisions before you select your contest prize. Make sure you have reviewed and decided the following:

—— Number and levels of prizes

—— Prizes or recognition for all entrants or just winners

—— Attractiveness, motivational factors, and appropriateness of prizes

—— Library logo prize, library related or not

—— Use of a celebrity or author

—— Recognition versus a tangible prize

—— Public relations value of the prize

—— Potential participant and winner satisfaction

Stickers	Food event for all	Coupons
Pins	Magnets	Calculators
Buttons	Discounts	Art work exhibited
Movie passes	Pencils/pens	Bookmarks
Ribbons	Lanyards	Wristbands
Certificates		

Figure 6-8. Samples of Low-Cost Premiums or Incentives for All Entrants

1. Oriental Trading Company—sells a wide variety of inexpensive prizes by the dozens or 100s.

2. ALA Graphics—good source of quality library-themed items

3. Local Odd Lots, Big Lots, or other deep-discount variety stores— sell unusual items inexpensively, but no standard stock and hard to predict what will be available

4. Sam's Club, Costco, or other large-scale wholesale clubs—sell things in bulk, can often be the source for inexpensive prizes

5. Janway Company, Amsterdam Printing, National Pen Corporation—good sources for affordable logo items

Figure 6-9. Places to Obtain Inexpensive Prizes

7 CHOOSE JUDGES AND SET JUDGING CRITERIA

The rules for the contest have been set, and the prize has been carefully chosen. At this point in the planning process, it is time to decide who will be judging the contest and on what factors the judge or judges will be basing their decisions. It is important to note here that many library contests do not require any type of judging. Contests to guess the number of something, drawings, trivia contests (in which only scoring is required), and many summer reading contests (where winning or completing the contest depends solely on the number of books read or hours spent reading) are all examples of contests that do not require a judge or judging. If this is the type of contest you or your team is planning, then it is fine to skip ahead to Step Eight in the planning process, Promote the Contest.

However, if your contest will require some type of judging, your team will not only have to choose the judge or judges for the contest, they will also have to establish criteria for judging entries. Both of those tasks require thoughtful consideration, always keeping in mind the contest goals. For instance, if the contest goal is to increase participation in library activities by twelve-year-old boys, the judge needs to be someone with some knowledge of how twelve-year-old boys act, what their interests are, and what kind of entries might be expected. In keeping with that same example, the choice of the judge can actually help with the achievement of the goal. If baseball is a popular activity in the community for boys of that age, then a minor or major league player from the area could be a good choice for a judge, especially if the judge will be presenting the prizes in person.

Many times, the contest judge will be the library director or the contest planner. Other possibilities for contest judge could be the head of the library board, a corporate sponsor, a PTA president, some city or county official, or some other influential person. For contests that require a high level of creative talent or technical skills, you need to select people whose talents match the type of contest. Working in partnership with the local community college, technical school, or college and university in the area is a good way to locate potential contest judges. It is important to recognize that in many smaller towns, people might be selected as judges because of their financial connection or their political connection rather than their technical skill level.

FACTORS TO CONSIDER IN SELECTING A JUDGE OR JUDGES

To help you and your team focus on this aspect of contest planning, take a few minutes as a group or individually to brainstorm answers to these key questions:

- What are the judging needs of the contest? Factors to consider here include the level of complexity of entries (will judges be reading 500-word essays or looking at photographs?), number of entries anticipated, and the contest schedule (how quickly do you need a decision?)

- What level of expertise is needed to judge entries? Will judging require a specific prior knowledge of or familiarity with a particular topic or art form, for example?

- What time commitment is required by the judge or judges? Is it just judging entries, or will the person be expected to be present at the awards presentation? Will there be media commitments?

- Is a single judge or a team of judges needed? Factors to consider here include the number of entries anticipated, location of entries (for example, if the entries are on display somewhere), and the sensitivity of the decision—especially with competition involving children, a team of judges prevents one person from being singled out as the "bad guy" for not choosing a particular child's entry as the winning one.

- Are there special circumstances to be considered? For example, if it is an election year, steer clear of using a single candidate or a seated public official running for re-election. If the contest has strong community partners or sponsors, will those people want to be involved in the judging or selection of judges?

- Can the type of judge chosen help in promotion of the contest? Although you will not address contest promotion in depth until you get to the next step in the planning process, it is not too early to be thinking about whether the choice of judge will help draw in more entries. Celebrity judges are always a big draw. Sometimes, using a judge who is an expert in a field related to the contest can attract more entries (such as a well-known poet judging a poetry contest).

The judge or judges chosen must be people who are perceived by potential entrants as fair, knowledgeable, and equitable. They must be people who can view the common good and do not have an outside agenda. Be careful in selection of a person to be a judge in a library contest who is "related to everyone around" in the community. Using political candidates in an election year is unadvisable, as is choosing a judge from a single faith organization. If a particular bank is your corporate partner, it would not be wise to choose as a judge someone who works for a rival bank. Selecting a judge or judges is a very important step but one that you need to make based on your best common sense.

SELECTING INDIVIDUALS

After you and your team have brainstormed answers to the specified questions, make a list of what qualities you are looking for and what expectations you have of a contest judge. Use this list to create a pool of possible candidates for the job. As you and your team consider the candidates for contest judge, keep in mind factors such as other activities going on during the scheduled time for the contest and whether or not a particular person on your list judges contests frequently, is judging another contest during the same time period, or has judged another contest fairly recently. If you are going to ask a prominent local author to judge a short story contest, make sure the contest is not in the middle of the person's upcoming book tour. Do not ask the basketball coach to judge the contest in the middle of the upcoming basketball tournament, and do not ask your library director to judge an essay contest the week the annual budget is due.

From the list of potential judges, divide the pool into first and second choices. This is the time for the contest-planning team to decide if there will be a single contest judge or a panel of judges. Your previous brainstorming session will guide you in making this determination. Prioritize your list for each category. Once your list is divided and prioritized and you know how many judges you need, simply work your way through the list. The next section outlines the process of contacting potential judges on your list.

CONTACTING POTENTIAL JUDGES

When talking with potential judges, clearly articulate what their duties, responsibilities, and time commitments will be. By being clear and covering all the bases at the start, you can help avoid confusion and questions later in the process. Whether you are asking the library director, the head coach of the college basketball team, or the mayor to judge the contest, there are certain questions that invariably will arise:

- What will I be judging?
- How many entries are anticipated?
- How long will it take?
- What will the judging involve?

Most people you talk to will want to have some idea not only of what a typical entry will consist of but also how many entries you think you will receive. Also, you need to estimate how long of a time commitment you expect the judge to make to the contest. Sometimes, the time commitment is minimal—selecting the prettiest pet, for example, rarely requires a great deal of effort. Other times, as in an essay contest, the time commitment is much greater. Finally, you should give the potential judge an idea of what you expect from him or her as far as the actual judging is concerned. Will the judge be expected to provide written comments on all entries? Will he or she be expected to present the prizes to the winners? Will the judge have to consider all entries or the group of entries comprising the final cut? Will they need to confer with the other judges to reach a consensus?

> **TIP:** Make the judge's role clear.

The method of contacting the judge or judges depends largely on who the person is and what the local community is like. There are times when a phone call or informal conversation is appropriate. This will most likely be the case when you, someone on your planning team, or someone on your staff or board knows the potential judge well. Other times, a more formal request, such as a letter or meeting with contest planners, makes sense. You may wish to send a letter to potential judges listing expectations and details about a specific contest. Whichever method you choose, make sure to state clearly what your expectations are. In order to do that fully, work through the next section of the chapter to set the judging criteria. When writing a letter to ask someone to judge your library contest, be sure to include all the important information while keeping the letter straightforward and to the point.

SETTING THE JUDGING CRITERIA

By its very nature, judging is somewhat subjective. After all, a judge is being asked to make a decision about which thing is the best, and that is going to involve some degree of that person's personal opinion. The key to making the contest judging process as even and fair to all as possible is to make sure the judge or judges know clearly at the start on what factors or criteria they should be basing their decisions. Those factors or judging criteria need to be in writing and distributed to the judges before the judging process begins.

The manner in which the library contest is scored depends largely on the philosophy of the contest planner based on the number of winners that may occur. If there is going to be only one winner, the prize is awarded to the person who achieves the highest level of performance. However, many contest designers believe that anyone who puts forth effort should be rewarded. The difference in these two philosophies is clearly indicated in the change in library summer reading programs over the last few decades. In the 1970s and 1980s, many programs were summer reading contests with prizes awarded only to children who read the highest number of books. In the late 1980s and into the early 1990s, however, many summer reading events changed from contests to programs. This change led to the nation-wide rise of the summer reading club or program with rewards to everyone who participates. This philosophy is acceptance of the idea that opportunity is not always equal and that participation or improved performance may be a more realistic basis for awarding reading contest prizes.

In making decisions about the judging, scoring methods, and criteria, there are several important factors to keep in mind:

- Age of entrants
- Contest scope
- Degree of complexity of entries

Discussion of these factors with the planning team will guide the formal establishment of the judging criteria. The judging criteria need to be diverse enough to separate one entry or group of entries from another, yet simple enough that the judge or judges can make easy, clear, and consistent determinations about each entry. Remember, the judging criteria are like a road map to find the contest winner. They need to be able to direct the judge or judges to a decision.

CRITERIA TO CONSIDER

The judge or judges chosen by the planner or planning team may have some input on the judging criteria, but it is important to have the criteria initially mapped out before even contacting the judges. The specificity of the criteria will change depending on the type of contest, but general criteria to use include the following:

- Originality—Does the entry express new ideas or look at the project from a different perspective? Are there entries that are very different from the others? If so, in what ways do these entries stand out? Do any of the entries do something unexpected?
- Adherence to the rules—Does the entry address the project guidelines? Are all entry requirements met satisfactorily? Does the entry fit the theme?
- Neatness—Is the entry typed or written legibly? Are elements of the entry arranged according to guidelines? Are they arranged logically? Are correct grammar and spelling used?

- Comprehensiveness—Does the entry fully cover the topic? Are all available resources used? Is the entry complete? Does it have a "finished" feel?

CRITERIA FOR SPECIFIC TYPES OF CONTESTS

Within each of these general categories the contest-planning team may want to add more specific criteria, especially if the contest requires entrants to display a particular skill. It is here that you may want to enlist the help of your chosen judges or experts in the field. The following list includes more specific criteria to consider for contests such as poetry, photography, sculpture, or essay contests:

- Art contests—Consider use of color, demonstration of technical skill, style, technique, originality, and use of materials.
- Essay contests—Consider grammar and spelling, demonstration of knowledge of theme or topic, adherence to essay topic, logical organization of ideas, and originality of focus.
- Creative writing contests—Consider adherence to specific genre requirements where applicable, freshness of imagery, overall originality, character and plot development for fiction, and image development for poetry.

Once you and your team have decided on the judging criteria to use for the contest, write them down. The list of criteria can then be given to judges as is or can be formalized into one of the types of scoring methods described in the next section of this chapter.

SCORING METHODS

Making the job a little easier for judges requires a bit of extra work on the part of contest planners. However, if you anticipate making contests a regular part of your library programming, the extra work is certainly worth the effort. There are two common scoring methods we will consider here: a point system and a rubric for ranking entries. Once you have set these up, you can always reuse them for future contests.

Library contest planners who choose to award merchandise, cash, or travel awards often find it helpful to set a scale of values for each contest objective that is achieved. If the library contest you are holding is art related, some factors you might want or need to score would include origi-

CRITERION	1—Strong	2—Good	3—Fair	Comments
Use of color: Was there an unusual or different use of color or juxtaposition of colors? Was there something that surprised or intrigued you?				
Neatness of entry: Even if not in the lines, was the coloring neat? Evenly applied? Was the paper neat, not wrinkled or torn?				
Originality: Did the child make use of unusual patterns, shading, mixing of colors?				
Use of other materials: Does the entry exhibit use of different types of coloring implements, like markers or colored pencils; application of glitter or other ornamentation?				
Use of different techniques: Were noticeable coloring techniques applied, such as a varying of pressure used with crayons, use of outlining, different types of shading, or mixing of crayons and paint?				

Figure 7-1. Sample Scoring Rubric

nality, relation of the entry to the contest goals, relevance of the entry to the theme, use of color, adherence to the rules, and aesthetic value. Using a point system with each of the items weighted helps the contest judge know what you are expecting. This type of scoring system can also help in awarding prizes. Some library contest designers set up a prize point system in which each prize must be valued in points. Each entrant's total score is computed, and prizes are awarded based on the accumulated number of points. If a contestant has earned 90–100 points, they can select a prize from the highest category; 80–89, the next highest; and so on. When the merchandise prizes are awarded, it is a sound strategy to offer a wide variety. More interest is generated in a contest when winners exercise their choice of prizes.

A less complex contest could benefit more from a simple judging rubric. To do this, decide what factors or criteria you want the judges to use, then make up a simple worksheet—often a half-page is sufficient—listing the criteria and asking for a ranking of 1, 2, or 3 for each one. Especially with a large number of entries, this process makes separating out the top entries a fairly quick and easy process. The judge can make piles of entries—all entries that have 1's for each criterion go in one pile, those that have mostly 1's with some 2's go in a second pile, those with no 1's go in a third pile, and so on. Once the top-ranked pile has been determined, the judge or judges can select the winner from a narrowed field. This method works well for a group of judges. Once each judge has ranked the entries by the use of the rubric, the group can get together and compare their ranked entries. Entries that are top ranked by each judge form the final pool from which to determine the winner.

CONCLUSION

The competitive nature of many contests means the contest judge or judges play a crucial role in the whole process. As you and your team move through this step in the contest-planning process, you may find that the judges you choose become committed partners in your library's overall programming. Some may even become new library patrons. Many people love to be asked to use their particular talents to help out a worthwhile organization like a library.

Further, setting clear judging criteria helps ensure a consistent, fair, and pleasurable experience for everyone involved. You may even decide to include the judging criteria in your contest promotional materials which will be discussed further in the next chapter. Even if a contestant does not win the contest this time around, he or she will know the areas to work on to improve for the next one.

8 PROMOTE THE CONTEST

As contest planner, you have made many important decisions to get ready to hold the contest. You are ready to go forward. Everything is in place, from entry forms to prizes and judges. The date is set to open the contest. Despite all of the best organizing and planning, if the contest is not promoted, people will not know about it, nor will they be motivated to enter. In promoting the contest, you are promoting the library.

This chapter outlines how to use a contest positively to increase goodwill for the library by using a contest as part of the public relations strategy. It also gives specific guidelines on promotional strategies for the contest itself. As you move through this step in the planning process, you will see how closely these two aspects of contest promotion are related. At times it is even difficult to distinguish one from the other. That is because they both have the same general purpose, which is to focus community attention on the library and its programs.

In order to establish a clearer understanding of what it means to promote the contest and to use the contest as part of a larger promotional effort, it is important to clarify some terms. You have probably heard the term *marketing* used in many situations. Even in the pages of this book, you have read about the importance of making a contest part of your library's marketing plan. You may even have a marketing department or marketing staff member in your own library. Marketing looks for opportunities to create growth and to expand the customer base. But what is marketing? To many people marketing is synonymous with public relations, advertising, promotion, and sales. Marketing is more than all of these strategies.

Often these four terms are used interchangeably. It is important to have a basic understanding of the terms before discussing how contests fit into an advertising campaign, are a library promotion, and are a part of the overall library marketing plan or a public relations strategy. None of these terms is a new concept. The term *advertising* dates back to 1807, but *marketing* was first used in 1561. *Contest* is the earliest word of all, tracing its origin to the early 1500s.

DEFINITION OF TERMS

Lisa Wolfe's *Library Public Relations, Promotions, and Communications: A How-To-Do-It-Manual* nicely shows the distinctions among these four terms:

1. "Advertising—Calling something to the attention of the public, especially by paid announcements.
2. Promotion—Trying to further the growth or development of something, trying to sell through advertising, publicly or discounting.
3. Marketing—1. Actually selling or purchasing in a market. 2. A combination of functions involving moving goods from producer to consumer.
4. Public Relations—The business of trying to convince the public to have understanding for a goodwill toward a person, firm, or institution; also, the degree of understanding and goodwill achieved."*

LIBRARIES AND PROMOTION

Some libraries were late to adopt techniques and concepts of promoting themselves and their work, thinking instead that the library was "a public good" and it was not necessary to "sell" the library. Going back in library history, one of the reasons that libraries changed from subscription libraries and private libraries was the great clamoring for the written word and the books that contained a wide range of ideas. In the 1930s when public libraries were seen as the poor man's university, all the seats in the libraries were full. Students in high school and college viewed visits to the library as an integral part of their education and did not need incentives to get them to use the library. In many schools, visits to the library were required.

As society became more complex, as public media outlets expanded, as competition to provide similar services became more competitive, all types of agencies, both public and private, came to understand the need to sell, promote, advertise, and market their product.

---

* Lisa A. Wolfe, *Library Public Relations, Promotions, and Communications: A How-To-Do-It Manual* (New York: Neal-Schuman Publishers, 2005), p. 43.

John Cotton Dana, librarian at the Newark Public Library, was one of the first librarians to use promotional strategies in a major way. He is widely recognized as the father of library public relations. The John Cotton Dana Library Public Relations Award of the American Library Association, sponsored by the H.W. Wilson Company, has been awarded since 1946 and has as its goal "to honor outstanding library public relations, whether a summer reading program, a year-long centennial celebration, fundraising for a new college library, an awareness campaign, or an innovative partnership in the community."*

What has become clear as the services provided by libraries have continued to increase and as their function has continued to expand and change is that the idea of marketing the library correspondingly has become more complex. All of the concepts—marketing, promotion, advertising, and public relations—are interrelated. One cannot exist without the other.

So how do library contests fit into the mix, and what role do they play in the library's marketing plan? Contests can fit into each concept. A contest can be a public relations tool. It can help people understand a certain service of the library or add to the goodwill a person feels about the library. A library contest can help sell or market a service of the library. A library contest can promote the growth and development of an aspect of library service. A library contest can be the feature that you choose to advertise and use to call attention to a unique service of the library. Because a library contest can be used in many ways, it is helpful to identify which areas of your library's marketing plan the use of a contest fits. Are you trying to create goodwill with the contest? Are you trying to feature or promote a particular service or library feature with the contest? Are you trying to raise awareness of the library? The contest will have better overall results if you first have thought through its part in your overall library strategies. Let us explore a library contest's role in each concept of public relations, marketing, advertising, and promotion.

> **TIP:** Consider entering your contest and its promotion for a John Cotton Dana Award.

PROMOTION AND CONTESTS

The contest planner or planning team needs to plan contest promotion early and match the strategy to the contest goals. The marketing department in a large or medium-sized library may be totally in charge of promotion, and the contest planner just needs to keep in contact with the marketing department. In a school, publicity might need to be vetted through a department head, principal, or head office. In a college or university, the staff

* Web site of the H.W. Wilson Co.: www.hwwilson.com/jcdawards/nw_jcd.htm.

responsible for promotion might not be located in the library. Remember that promotion is trying to further the growth or development of something. The Friends of the Erie County Public Library in Erie, Pennsylvania, held an adult summer reading contest based on a game of Bingo to promote Books I Never Got O-Round To (see Figure 8-1). In order to be eligible for a prize, contestants had to have read in specific categories, such as classics, memoir, inspiration, a magazine you had never read, One Book—One Erie, and true crime. This contest encouraged people to read in areas they did not usually read in. Contestants had to listen to an audio book, too, so it helped to promote the library's expanding audio book collection.

Advertising can be part of any contest. Often a sponsor such as a newspaper, radio, or TV will donate or give discounted rates. Many radio stations will give free time to public service announcements which could involve information on your contest. When you are recruiting your sponsors or partners, make sure you have media outlets on your list to contact.

Public relations is the act of trying to convince the public to have goodwill toward the library. When you are introducing a new service, you are asking the public to embrace and use the service. A contest can easily be worked into a public relations campaign. The Johnson County Library in Overland Park, Kansas, held a bookmark contest to honor the fiftieth anniversary of the Friends of the Library. They wanted to encourage people to appreciate and have goodwill toward the Friends and the library. Entrants could check a box to receive more information about the Friends. This a good use of a contest to gather information for another promotional purpose, to expand the membership of the Friends of the Library. The bookmark design was to "show how the library is your friend, how the library has helped you, how librarians are your friends, or how you can be a friend to the library." In addition to designing a bookmark, people had to write a paragraph about "How the Johnson County Library Is Your Friend or How You Can Be a Friend to the Library." The entire contest was about promoting goodwill for the Friends and the library.

LOCAL PUBLICITY

One of the biggest and most prevalent reasons for holding a library contest is the publicity value of such an event. Even if you do not have a lot of participants, even if you do not have all the kinks worked out, it is an event that involves the public, and thus it is more newsworthy than the usual day-to-day library business of checking out books, attending weekly story times, and using the computer. In her *Clever Contests That Will Tempt Reporters to Call*, Joan Stewart says that contests are valuable publicity tools primarily because you can create publicity before, during, and after the contest with press releases, timed announcements, and special events connected to them. "They provide an aura of suspense," she writes. "And they're one of

Erie County Public Library
Adult Summer Reading Program

B I N G -O

Books I Never Got O-Round To

Biography	Romance	Short Story Collection	Poetry	Classic
Mystery	One Book One Erie	Western	Current Issues	Any Audio Book
True Crime	Travel	Your Choice	A Magazine You Have Never Read	Adventure
Read To a Child	Inspiration	Health	Historical Fiction	Horror or Suspense
Science Fiction	Humor	How To	Detective Fiction	Memoir

Name ________________ Phone ________________

When completed, return to any Library outlet, by the end of August for a chance in a prize drawing!

Figure 8-1. Erie County Bingo Card
(Used by permission of librarian staff at the Erie County Public Library.) (*Continued on page 130*)

Rules and procedures:

The Adult Summer Reading Program runs from June through August and is open to readers age 15 and up. Library employees and persons living in their households are welcome to participate, but ineligible for the grand prize drawings.

Pick up your Bingo card at the Information Hub at the Blasco Library or any branch library. Complete your card by filling in adjacent squares to make a solid row across, up and down, or diagonal. Each square on the card requires a separate book. Only books that are read during the program dates (June through August) can be used to make a Bingo. The books must be read, except if you use the 'Any Audio Book' square. Also, an audio book can be used for the 'Your Choice' square. Write the title and author of the book you have read in the appropriate space.

Bring your completed card to the Bingo Box at the Information Hub at the Blasco Library or the Branch libraries. You may request another card at that time. There is a limit of ten cards. Completed Bingo cards will be entered for a prize drawing in September.

The Friends of the Erie County Public Library
is the major sponsor of the
Adult Summer Reading Program.

Here's a brief description of some of the categories:

Adventure - Select any book that recounts an exciting, unusual, or hazardous undertaking.

Any Audio Book - Listen to any book recorded on cassette or CD.

Biography - Read about an actor, athlete, musician, president, or any other luminary whose fame exceeded 15 minutes.

Classic - Choose a novel that has stood the test of time.

Current Issues - Read current thought on issues pertaining to education, politics, law, etc.

Health - Any health-related topic including biographies and history.

How To - Read about anything you would like to learn to do.

Humor - Fiction or nonfiction, if it makes you laugh its humor.

Inspiration - Read an uplifting fiction or non-fiction book.

Memoir - Written in the first person, a memoir focuses on a specific event, time, or place.

One Book One Erie - Ask a Library Staff member for the title of this year's One Book One Erie.

Poetry - Choose a book of poems by a single author, or an anthology.

Read to a Child - Find the right book, the right child, and enjoy.

Romance - Choose from books shelved in the Romance collection or visit www.escapetoromance.com for more suggestions.

Short Stories - Choose a collection of short stories by a single author, or look for a collection of stories by multiple authors.

Travel - Any fiction or non-fiction book in which travel is the main theme.

Western - Choose a book shelved in the western collection, or choose any book about pioneer life and westward expansion.

Erie County Public Library

160 East Front Street
Erie PA 16507
814-451-6927

REFERENCE@ERIELIBRARY.ORG
HTTP://WWW.ERIELIBRARY.ORG

**Figure 8-1. Erie County Bingo Card
(Used by permission of librarian staff at the Erie County
Public Library.)** (*Continued from page 129*)

the best ways to get publicity for your company without having to spend money on a paid ad."*

Many contests have a *product* associated with them—something that is produced as a result of the contest. It may be as simple as an entry form, a completed trivia contest answer sheet, a photo, or an essay. Or the product may be as complex as the actual construction of something—costumes made from duct tape, Web sites, or even murals inside or outside your building. Regardless of the product, chances are it was produced by someone from the community, and that in itself often makes it worthy of a news story—or at least a photo or news clip.

Other contests may feature *acquired items*. These might include things people bring from home or even things people need to seek and find. An example of a highly successful contest involving such an acquired item took place at the Tuckahoe Public Library in Westchester County, New York, as part of its 1995 summer reading program. The contest was part of a well-planned program organized around an interesting theme that doubled attendance at the summer reading program of this community library. The contest was called the Pretty Piggy Bank Contest—A Beauty Contest for the Fairest Piggy Bank in the Land. Children were invited to bring their piggy banks from home to stay at the library throughout the summer. The banks were numbered and placed in display cases.**

These are the types of things the local news media love because they bring with them the notion of a "photo op." A picture paints a thousand words, and everyone loves to see themselves in the newspaper or on TV.

NATIONAL PUBLICITY

Publicity on a national level is not a priority for most public libraries because most patronage and funding are generated at the local and state levels. However, there are times when contests at the local level can give an individual library or library system a voice in the national public forum. This type of involvement in something larger in scale can have a lot of benefit for local libraries. Positive national publicity for small and mid-size cities and towns can help build community pride, and when the local library becomes the focal point of that community pride, it can be a value for the library.

The Springfield (Massachusetts) City Library saw the value of this type of activity back in the mid-1980s when it hosted a four-month-long celebration of "Seussamania," cleverly capitalizing on its distinction of being located in the hometown of Dr. Seuss himself, Theodor Geisel. The

* Joan Stewart, *Clever Contests That Will Tempt Reporters to Call*, 2003, www.101public relations.com, 4.
** Elizabeth Sachs, "There's a Pig in the Library!" *School Library Journal*, April 1996, 44.

novelty of the program drew close to 30,000 young people and spurred a 50 percent system-wide increase in the circulation of children's books.* The Springfield Seussamania program was successful for several key reasons:

- It capitalized on unique local resources.
- It involved many community groups, from schools to private companies and the Friends of the Library.
- It included multiple activities centered on a single theme—activities that included reading and trivia contests as well as musical and dramatic performances and art exhibits.

In the 1980s, this well-conceived and well-executed program was a novelty for a public library system. Today, Seussamania programs are held on Dr. Seuss's birthday across the country in libraries and schools, and Springfield itself continues to play a key role in those celebrations.

Not every library has the resources or the proper context to generate such an initiative on its own, but participating in programming of this nature as part of a collective can be of considerable advantage. Participating in such a national forum and getting publicity in the national media, in library-oriented publications and popular media, offers the added benefit of publicity among libraries in general. This type of publicity opens the door to the sharing of knowledge, experiences, and in some cases even resources. In a sense, this strengthens libraries across the board—what is good for one is good for all.

The announcement of the contest can be a media event, and depending on the theme and its relevance, there might be a feature story you can create ahead of time. During the contest, a news item might be constructed around the number of entries received. The contest winner recognition event can be a newsworthy event and a photo opportunity. If the contest results in an exhibit of some kind, the press should be interested in covering it. Many times, you can also promote a feature story on the winners. Even if no one from the press is there for the actual winner announcement, be sure to capture the moment digitally to send to the newspaper with a press release.

PROMOTIONS

Throughout this book are many examples of contest promotions. There is no one right way to promote a contest, but the contest planner needs to stimulate interest throughout the contest. If you hold a contest for staff, you would want to send out an e-mail message or post information on the bulletin board or

* " 'Seussamania' in Geisel's Hometown," *American Libraries*, June 1986, 485.

use the school's morning announcements to arouse the curiosity of possible entrants. The contest announcement itself has not gone out yet, but the note suggests something important is about to happen. The contest announcement's purpose is for notification and to generate enthusiasm. There should be reminders to maintain interest in the contest. Each library needs to determine the promotional methods that will work best for that library. Use the sample form in Figure 1-1 on page 3 to help create a planning document for your own contest. Planning the timeline can help make sure tasks get completed.

Promotional Methods

The promotional aspect of your contest is actually the place where all the other factors discussed thus far come together. Contest promotion must take into account audience, scheduling, theme, type, prizes, and entry requirements. The type and level of coverage of your promotion are determined by money invested, library contacts, and word-of-mouth connections. Different promotional methods vary in cost and whom they reach. The following list identifies some of the most frequently used promotional methods:

Promotional pieces:

- Bookmarks
- Flyers
- Community bulletin board notices
- Posters
- Press releases
- Contest entry brochure
- Library calendar
- Direct mail
- Billboards
- Bus or subway placards
- Restaurant placemats

Newspapers:

- News articles
- Features
- Editorials
- Announcements
- Advertisements

Radio:

- Public service announcements
- Talk show interviews
- Advertisements

Television:

- Public service pieces
- Interviews
- Tie-ins with local programming

Computer:

- Library Web site
- Blogs
- Links from partner Web sites

Most contests will engender some type of media coverage whether it be school, university, or public library. The campus newspaper, the school Web site, or the local newspaper will have interest in the library's contest. The question is, how do you spark the media's interest in your contest? In many cases, it may be as simple as making a phone call to your local reporter. At times, a more formal press release to a list of radio, TV, and press contacts is more appropriate (see Figure 8-2). Do not overlook the possible connections to the media from your board and staff. Often a personal contact can get the job done when a more generic approach fails.

Using your library Web site for promotion is a cost-effective, easy method of getting the word out about your contest. Short, concise paragraphs describing the contest, rules, and even winners can easily reach a lot of people. With the number of people who use the Web as a major source of information growing every year, the significance of online promotion is also on the rise. You may even consider putting entry forms and vital links in your contest descriptions on the Web site.

A more traditional approach to promotion is the use of printed pieces, including posters, flyers, bookmarks, and the library's monthly calendar. Slipping a bookmark in every book that is checked out reaches the primary library audience. For the many libraries that continue to use direct mail as part of their distribution of the calendar of events, this avenue presents a timely method of contest promotion (see Figure 8-3). Posters and flyers can be inexpensive and easy to reproduce. They can be posted around town as well as in the library itself. Be sure to ask permission before posting flyers in public places.

Word-of-mouth advertising is a tried-and-true method of promotion.

Radio and TV PSA

For Immediate Release   *Contact: [YOUR NAME]*
[DATE]   *[YOUR PHONE]*

Annual Poster Contest Announced

Area 5th graders will get a chance to showcase their creative talents in the Annual Poster
Contest at the [YOUR LIBRARY NAME]. The contest officially begins on
[DAY/DATE OF CONTEST START] when official entry forms and submission
guidelines will be available at all library locations and on the library website [WEB
ADDRESS].

Last year, about 150 youngsters entered the contest, and an even bigger turnout is
expected this year. The theme of this year's contest is [THEME]. To enter, students will
have one month to create a poster illustrating the theme. The contest is being held in
partnership with [NAME OF LOCAL SCHOOL DISTRICT], and art teachers in the
elementary schools have agreed to help students with design elements and give them time
in class to work on the posters.

This year's top prize, sponsored by [NAME OF SPONSOR], is a $50 gift certificate and
a backpack filled with school supplies. Three Honorable Mention winners will also
receive the backpacks.

"This is a way for the public library and the local school district to join forces to
encourage kids' creativity and civic pride," said School Superintendent John Smith.

Library Director Mary Jones agreed. "We are all committed to providing our children
with the best possible educational opportunities, and this annual poster contest is an
example of what can be done when we work together."

**For more information or to schedule photo opportunities, please contact the
library's marketing department at [PHONE NUMBER]. You can also contact the
children's department [PHONE NUMBER] for details on the contest.**

**Figure 8-2. A Public Service Announcement (PSA) to local radio
and TV stations should include contest highlights, contact
information, and key information about the event. Reporters may
call the library for more information or to do a more detailed story,
or the TV or radio station may run the announcement just as it
was submitted. Try to put key details in the first paragraph in case
the stations decide to cut parts out of the rest of the release.**

Figure 8-3. Calendar Announcement
(Used by permission of Lexington Public Library, designed by Peggy McAllister, staff graphic artist.)

The beauty of word-of-mouth advertising is that it is free. Make sure your staff, student aides, board members, and volunteers are equipped with a clear, concise, and accurate summary of contest details. This will go a long way in making sure what is being spread by word of mouth is the message you want delivered.

Often your contest partners are able to spread the word about the contest through their own promotional channels, such as Web sites and newsletters. This, too, is at no cost to the library. Partners may also be engaged to help pay for advertisements in local media outlets or on billboards. For example, your local billboard company may be willing to donate empty billboard space for your contest promotion. This is a great way to involve the community and get your message out.

> **TIP:** You might have to promote outside the library to reach your target audience.

All of the aforementioned promotional strategies are good ways to reach general audiences. However, they might not necessarily reach the target audience the planning team identified in Step Three. Depending on the target audience that you want to reach, the contest-planning team should take a few minutes to brainstorm a list of possible locations and outlets outside the library where members of the target audience are likely to see promotional materials. Setting up a table at the local PTA meeting, Boys and Girls Club, grocery store, or newcomers' class is a way to get your message out to very specific segments of the community. Flyers placed in doctors' offices or hospital waiting rooms, grocery stores, pawnshops, movie theaters, and even restaurants could draw the attention of non–library users.

Promotion itself can be a contest goal. The Urbana Regional Public Library in Maryland formed a new Friends of the Urbana Regional Library in anticipation of their newest library opening in 2006. The group was looking for a logo to help promote the new library and Friends organization. They kept the design costs at zero as they partnered with a local high school art class to take the logo design on as a contest.

CONTEST WRAP-UP

Every successful contest has a well-planned wrap-up. Press conferences, awards presentations, or an exhibition of the winning works are all possible wrap-up activities. Participants, partners and sponsors, the media, and the community at large need to know when the contest is over and when the awards and prizes will be distributed. This does not mean your event needs to be fancy or involved. You can inexpensively and simply put together a cookie and juice reception and hold the awards ceremony right in the children's department or school gym. Add some colorful balloons, a display of all the entries, and some lively music, and you have a party that everyone will enjoy. On the other hand, you can make your awards ceremony a major

TIP: If your budget has no room in it for a fancy reception, remember, even $25 will go a long way at your local dollar store. Many of these have everything you need from colorful cups and napkins to helium balloons and cookies.

event for your library, school, or college. This is a great time to get community partners and volunteer organizations (like your Friends or PTOs) involved. Regardless of complexity, the wrap-up creates clear closure for the contest and offers a terrific vehicle for publicity for your library.

The annual Snyder Book Collecting Contest organized by the University of Kansas Libraries and Oread Books began in 1957 (see Figure 8-4). The top prize that first year was $75, and about twenty students entered. Today the contest draws a much larger entry pool with divisions for both graduate and undergraduate students. The contest wraps up each year with a formal awards presentation program and reception.

FINALIZING THE BUDGET

You worked diligently to estimate your budget in Step Two. Since you have made all the major planning decisions about your contest, it is now time to return to your estimated budget and refine it. Try to be as accurate as you can with your budget, keeping in mind that you might be called on to share the information with your partners, potential funders, and others involved in the contest. A little extra work at this point in the planning process will save you work down the road. Accurate budgeting before you start the contest keeps you and your planning team on the right track financially. It would be detrimental to the contest not to have enough money to finish the good work you have begun.

CONCLUSION

The last chapter in this book outlines sample contests, working through each step in the planning process, including how each contest lets people know about it. The promotional methods are varied, and there are many paths to success. Choose the one that works for you.

If you would like additional information about formulating a promotional plan for your contest or other library activities, there are many excellent books that can offer detailed help in promotion, public relations, and marketing. A contest should be part of your overall marketing plan, so it would be helpful to review several books on marketing before you get started.

The first book is *Library Public Relations, Promotions, and Communications* by Lisa A. Wolfe, Neal-Schuman #75, 1997, which "provides an

introduction to the basic communications concepts, a step-by-step process for developing and implementing a library public relations/communication plan, and descriptions of effective library communication tools and strategies." The second book is *Library Marketing That Works!* by Suzanne Walters, Neal-Schuman, 2004, which "examines marketing as a process through which we come to understand our customers." It offers practical, step-by-step guidance from concept through development and implementation of a library marketing plan. Finally, *Powerful Public Relations: A How-To Guide for Libraries*, edited by Rashelle S. Karp, offers some excellent specific examples of promotional pieces such as PSAs and news releases along with guides to creating documents for a variety of library programs, including exhibit applications and photo releases.

9 EVALUATE SUCCESS

You and your planning team have already checked off most of your contest planning to-do list. One final planning task remains: evaluation. You may be wondering why evaluation is the final step of the contest plan when it does not take place until after the contest is over. In reality, evaluation is a necessary part of the plan because it must be considered throughout all the steps of the contest plan. It is closely connected with goals, promotion, budget, and partnerships. Evaluation may even be thought of as the glue that holds the plan together. If you plan to evaluate how many people participated in the contest and your goal is to involve a specific number of people, you need to plan early on how to track that so you can measure at the end if you actually met your goal.

The importance of evaluation in any program or project cannot be overestimated, especially in this country, where most of us were brought up on grades, test scores, and report cards only to graduate to performance evaluations, customer satisfaction surveys, and market research questionnaires. Evaluation is the way many people achieve closure on projects in their lives. Evaluation offers a way to move fluidly from one project to the next, from one job to another, even from quarter to quarter and year to year. Corporations make regular periodic evaluation of every aspect of their work a part of business as usual. Last quarter, earnings were down. This quarter we expect to improve those numbers. Last year was a banner growth year for us, and this year we plan to build on that growth and take our company to the next level.

So it is with library contests. Every contest needs to be evaluated to determine several important factors:

- Did the contest achieve its goals?
- What was the cost of the contest including staff time, in-kind services, donations, and actual cash spent?
- What was the value of the contest?
- Should the contest be held again?
- What worked, and what did not?
- What specific gains did the contest generate? Did circulation increase? Did more people use the library's new service? How many patrons came through the doors because of the contest?

• What adjustments can we make to improve the project for the next time?

KEYS TO VALUABLE EVALUATION

Useful evaluative tools are a smooth blend of quantitative assessment—the numbers—and qualitative assessment—the more subjective opinion portion. They also mix standard questions used for every program to achieve consistency with those tailored specifically to the project. They need to correspond with the contest goals the planning team established early in planning process. One size does *not* fit all when it comes to evaluation, and you must be prepared for the fluid nature of successful and useful evaluation tools. Evaluation tools that do not offer program planners and partners anything concrete or useful are a waste of everyone's time.

Here are a few keys to creating useful project evaluations:

• Bring all partners into the evaluative process. Evaluation tools may differ. Community partners may be asked to evaluate only the partnership aspect or a specific event tied to the contest. Library staff involved in the project may be asked to evaluate the partnerships themselves as well as the overall outcome. Together they form a complete and useful assessment of the project outcomes.

• Tie evaluation tools directly to the planning process. This avoids overgeneralization in the evaluation process. For example, it is more helpful to assess how well the contest met your circulation increase goal than it is to ask, "Was the contest a success?" In addition, you should have your evaluation tools (forms, interview questions, statistics needed) prepared before you hold the contest. By doing this, you will know what data to collect throughout the project, which can help in making your entry forms.

• Do not save evaluation until the end. Throughout the project—however long or short it may be—periodically review your initial goals and your progress toward achieving them. This can really help bolster enthusiasm, even in the midst of what seems to be a sinking ship. For example, you may be halfway through your summer reading program and entries are down 25 percent from where they were the previous summer at that point. You and your staff may be disheartened by the figures, but when you revisit your initial goals for the program, you find that one of your main goals was to increase circulation of children's materials by 20 percent and your circulation stats for that month already show a 15 percent rise. The point is, that while entries may be down, you are already well on the way to achieving one of your primary goals for the project, and so it is already a success.

SPECIFIC EVALUATION TOOLS

The type of evaluation tools you choose to use depends largely on the type and amount of information you want or need. If your contest involved community partners or was funded in part or in full through a grant or by the PTA, for instance, you may need to gather different demographic data than if you were evaluating a contest whose cost was covered entirely by the library. If this was your first attempt at a contest, you might want your evaluation tools to stress what happened in the process. You might be more interested in concentrating on what aspects worked smoothly and what parts were more problematic than you would be in knowing the exact ages of the contestants, because you are trying to build a foundation for future contests.

Let us look at some of the different evaluation tools typically used in projects of this nature. Remember, these tools can be used independently or in combination with each other. Additionally, you may want to use specific tools for specific groups involved. For instance, you may want your contest partners or sponsors to fill out a simple form, but you might want to hold an interview with sample participants. The best evaluation involves everyone who was a part of the contest. Whatever methods you choose, keep in mind these two key principles:

> **TIP:** Evaluation helps you and your team bring the contest to a natural end.

- Know ahead of time what information you want to gather
- Do the evaluation as soon as possible after the project is completed

END-OF-CONTEST MEETINGS

You have probably heard of this type of evaluation tool before, although it may have been called something slightly different. People in the theatre may call it a cast party. In the military, one might be a part of a debriefing. Whatever you call it, this type of evaluation basically involves bringing your key players together and talking about what happened during the project.

The setting and tone for these meetings also varies. A potluck dinner, for instance, is a great informal way to get everyone together to assess the project. This type of end-of-contest meeting is good for gaining a more general sense of the success of the project or at least of what pieces were the most successful. If your project was very large and involved a lot of people, this type of meeting allows everyone to get together, relax, and decompress. It brings a great sense of closure to a project that was complex or that took place over a long period of time. If you want to provide the refreshments for the evaluation party, include the cost in your overall budget at the beginning so that you know the money will be there at the end of the contest.

A downside to this type of evaluation is that information gathered can be quite general. Conversation at the dinner table or in a crowded room is difficult to track and document, and people tend to talk in general about all aspects of the project rather than focusing on the specific areas for which you are trying to generate information.

If you want to keep a tighter control on this type of evaluation tool, you may choose instead to hold an actual meeting in one of your meeting rooms, your boardroom, or even a "neutral" space at a hotel or community center, especially if you have a wide variety of partners and sponsors involved. This type of evaluation is very useful in gathering specific qualitative data. It is not a good way to gather numbers and demographic data.

Keys to making this type of evaluation work well include using a moderator and a note-taker, having a specific list of questions prepared ahead of time, and limiting both the amount of time and the number of people involved. Usually, people are not going to have the patience to sit and concentrate for more than an hour or hour and a half. The number of people in attendance should not exceed about twenty. More than that around the table makes it difficult to hear and difficult for everyone to have a chance to talk.

Another end-of-contest meeting option you might want to try is the off-site meeting. It is usually limited to twelve or fifteen people and held somewhere out of the line of fire for the typical workday distractions like telephones and computers. Another option is holding a number of small meetings, often lunch meetings with four or five people.

> **TIP:** Share initial results from the contest with those attending the evaluation meeting before they come.

INTERVIEWS

The key to making interviews work as an evaluation tool is keeping them simple. Too many questions in an interview can spell disaster for the interviewer and the subject. Five to ten well-thought-out questions certainly should suffice for any evaluative interview. Remember, this is not a legal deposition. It is an attempt to find out how the contest worked.

Who are the best candidates for evaluative interviews? Often it is the contest participants themselves who can give you the best feedback here. Decide how many people you want to interview, then think about whom you want to focus on. Perhaps you want a random sampling. In this case, you might arbitrarily ask every tenth entrant to answer a few questions for you. Or you may want to try to put together a representative sampling. In this case, decide what areas of representation you want to compile. For example, you might want three women, three men, two teenagers, and two senior citizens. You can identify areas of representation based on just about any demographic.

Putting together useful interview questions can be an entire project in itself. To minimize the amount of time you spend on this, Figure 9-1 lists some possible areas to cover in interview questions.

Participant satisfaction or dissatisfaction

Success or failure of particular marketing techniques

Popularity of prizes and premiums

Reasons for participation   Anticipation of future participation

Favorite parts or features   Ease of entry and participation

Areas for possible improvement

Figure 9-1. Possible Areas to Cover in End-of-Contest Interviews

A key to constructing useful interview questions is to make them broad-based enough to elicit some input yet narrow enough to keep the interviewee on topic. Coming up with good interview questions is like being Goldilocks trying the porridge in the story of Goldilocks and the Three Bears: Papa Bear's porridge was too hot and Mama Bear's porridge was too cold, but Baby Bear's porridge was just right. You want your interview questions to be just right. One note: avoid Yes or No questions whenever possible, unless you are planning a follow-up, like Why? or Why not? Figure 9-2 lists some questions that might help in your contest evaluations.

- What was your favorite part of the contest?
- How did you find out about the contest?
- What would you have done differently if you were running the show?
- Did any of your friends or family participate?
- How did you do?
- When we have this contest again next year, will you enter?
- What was the hardest part of the contest?
- What was the easiest part of the contest?
- What types of contests do you usually enter?
- What did you think about the prizes?
- What other kinds of contests would you enjoy at the library?
- Was this your first time entering a contest at the library?
- Why did you decide to participate?
- We're trying to get even more people to participate next year, what could we do to get more people to sign up?

Figure 9-2. Possible End-of-Contest Interview Questions

EVALUATION FORMS

Evaluation forms are probably the most common evaluative tool. Evaluation forms are in evidence everywhere, from customer satisfaction cards on the tables of restaurants or bedside tables in hotel rooms to online survey forms sent immediately after making a purchase on the Web. Any employer will likely have had to fill out an evaluation form on one of their employees or on themselves. Grant recipients must fill out final reports, students in colleges and universities across the country rate their professors, and all of us have received surveys of one kind or another from market research companies looking for our opinions on the quality and utility of every kind of product from dish soap to diapers.

Evaluation forms come in five basic varieties: short answer, narrative, rating, financial, and combination. Each variety has its own merits and drawbacks. Short answer forms, for instance, are quick for people to fill out, and they are good for getting specific information. The scope of the feedback is limited, however. Figure 9-3 offers an example of what such a form might look like. Narrative forms, on the other hand, take more time for evaluators to fill out, but they offer a much more detailed analysis (see Figure 9-4). This type of evaluation might be best used for the people involved in staging the contest rather than the contest entrants themselves. A rating form is another example of one that is quick to complete (see Figure 9-5). Like the short answer form, the scope is limited, but well-constructed questions can still elicit some useful evaluative information. This type of evaluation works well with children and teens.

1. How many contest entries did you have? _____

2. What were the ages of entrants?

      0–6 years old: _____

      7–12 years old: _____

      13–18 years old: _____

      19–35 years old: _____

      36–55 years old: _____

      56 years +: _____

3. Do you feel the contest was a success? Why? _____
_____
_____

4. Is there anything you would do differently next time? _____
_____

5. How many staff members worked on this contest? _____

6. How many volunteers or community partners? _____

7. Did this contest have any sponsorship from outside the library (local businesses, individuals, Friends of the Library)? If so, please list:
_____
_____
_____

8. How many prizes or premiums were awarded? _____

9. Do you plan to do the contest again next year? _____

10. Did you have any news coverage or publicity? _____

    Please attach clippings, posters, etc. to this form.

Figure 9-3. Washington County Public Library Battle of the Books Contest Evaluation

Financial forms are fairly specific in their use. Program sponsors, contest planners, and contest committee treasurers are the best people to complete these types of evaluations. You may see this referred to as a budget form or report, and good ones will factor in expenses and revenues, in-kind and actual. Financial forms can offer an excellent quantitative assessment of your contest.

You will most likely find that combination forms work the best. These forms may have a rating section and a narrative section, for instance. For your most comprehensive evaluation, you may want to develop a form for each of the major groups involved. You could have one form for contest participants, one for organizers and staff, and one for community partners or sponsors.

Once the evaluation is completed, the next task is analyzing the results. Your use of the results can be as important as the evaluation itself.

1. What was the response of students to the contest? Teachers? Parents?

2. What publicity activities did you do? What worked best? What didn't work?

3. Who were the key players in the project? List specific staff, departments, branches, community partners. Were there enough people involved? Too many? Why?

4. What were the most successful components of the contest? Why?

5. What didn't work? How do you plan to change things for the next contest?

Please attach any press clippings, promotional materials, and letters of support and/or commendation.

Figure 9-4. Southside Elementary School Second Annual Photo Contest Evaluation

WHAT TO DO WHEN THE CONTEST FAILS

As a library contest planner, that is probably a question you do not want to consider. In fact, many people would urge avoiding thoughts of this nature to keep the contest team's positive momentum going. The truth is, however, that the possibility of failure exists and, indeed, contests do fail. One of the keys to dealing with this possibility is choosing carefully your criteria for success during the planning stages. Having only a dozen people enter your major annual two-month-long photography contest may appear as failure on the face of it, but depending on the criteria you have chosen to meet your goals, you can also view it as a success. Those contestants may all be new library patrons, for example. Or maybe they have overcome great personal challenges even to be able to enter the contest. Success is often in the eye of the beholder. Even if your contest fails, no matter how you look at it, do not despair. Use your failures as learning opportunities. If it is your first contest, try to determine what worked and did not work so that you have a better chance of success with the next one. If you have had a successful run of a particular type of contest, then have had one that totally flops, consider

Central Library Annual Trivia Challenge
EVALUATION FORM

Please rate your experience with the Trivia Challenge using the following scale:

5 = Excellent
4 = Good
3 = Average
2 = Needs Improvement
1 = Substandard

	Excellent				Substandard
Difficulty of questions	5	4	3	2	1
Room set-up	5	4	3	2	1
Sound System	5	4	3	2	1
Refreshments	5	4	3	2	1
Event publicity	5	4	3	2	1
Contest prizes	5	4	3	2	1
Door prizes	5	4	3	2	1

Would you participate in Central Library Trivia Challenge again? YES   NO

Comments: _____

_____

How did you find out about this event? (Circle all that apply)

Newspaper   Radio   Flyers in library   From a friend   Participated last year

Anything else you'd like to share?

_____

_____

Thank you for your input!

Figure 9-5. Sample Contest Rating Form

the possibility that your community may be changing. Perhaps the interest in a particular type of program or activity has run its course, in which case you can begin brainstorming new ideas.

To avoid the general demoralization that can attend failure, keep the emphasis on your achievements, no matter how small. Remind your team that the contest was a group effort and that no individual is totally responsible for either the success or failure of the project. Use the momentum of the failure to begin planning for the next contest, being as detailed as possible about what worked and what did not. Finally, remind your team that this time's failure will only make next time's success that much sweeter.

HOW TO BUILD ON A SUCCESS

Use the momentum of your success to get people on board for the next contest. This needs to be done as soon as possible after you have wrapped up your project. You can give everyone a week or so to enjoy the fruits of their labor, but any longer than that and the excitement begins to fade. Here are some things to do in order to keep your success rolling right along:

- Designate or appoint a contest planner for the next contest. You are much more likely to have someone step up to take the reins of a program with an established success record. This is true whether you are working with community partners and volunteers or your own staff. Everyone wants to be a winner, which, of course, is part of what makes contests so popular.

- If you were working with a committee, appoint the new one. Because everyone will be glowing from the success, your new committee very likely will retain many members from the current one. Also, others who were peripherally involved may express an interest to join your efforts. Take them up on any offers to help.

- If you are working solely with library staff members, set some goals and priorities for the next contest right away. If you can get your people to buy into the goals early on, they are much more likely to sustain an interest throughout the year.

- If possible, try to pick the next contest theme or title. This is probably a lot easier than it may sound at first. Chances are, you will have received some input along these lines from your participants. You can also ask for suggestions for upcoming contests on your evaluation forms. The earlier you can start planning, the better. A theme or title really serves to focus that early planning.

- Set up a timeline, even if the next event is a year away. It is important to keep people working while they are excited about the project. The old adage holds true here, "Out of sight, out of mind," so keep everyone connected and involved. Make assignments tied to time goals and hold everyone accountable. Wouldn't it be nice to have all your prizes and graphics for your next contest done three or four months before it starts? Just imagine how much easier you will sleep at night not worrying about last-minute details.

CONCLUSION

Evaluation is a three-part process: First, you create your evaluation tools; second, you have participants complete them; and third, you analyze the information and report the results to the planners. Taking the time to complete a thorough evaluation of your contest may seem onerous at the time, especially when you feel you have invested all your creative energy in actually planning and holding the contest. However, the benefits of good evaluation are more than worth the time it takes to do it. You lighten the load for the person who will be organizing the next contest (which may, in fact, be you). You and your team can sit back and objectively look at your work, your patrons, and your library services, find points of intersection, and think creatively about contests and programs for the future.

10 NOW, PUT THE PLAN IN MOTION: FOUR MODEL CONTESTS

As you have perused the pages of this book, you have moved through all the steps involved in planning, implementing, and evaluating a library contest. Contests can be as simple or complex as those involved want to make them. However, regardless of the size of your library or how much staff time and financial resources are available, a contest can become a part of your library programming. Making a workable plan and then putting that plan in motion will help ensure the success of the contest.

The key in effective planning is moderation. Have a good, solid plan in place before you start, but remain flexible enough throughout the project to change the plan if the need presents itself. Keep all people involved in the contest—both staff and participants—informed about changes that occur, but encourage everyone to stick to the game plan and the rules to ensure the most enjoyment by the most people.

In this chapter, we will follow several contests from start to finish, using the planning steps established in the Introduction: (1) select the contest planner and consider community partnerships; (2) establish the contest goals and estimate the budget; (3) define the contest type, audience, and theme; (4) determine eligibility criteria and rules; (5) schedule the contest; (6) select the prize; (7) select judges and set judging criteria; (8) promote the contest; and (9) evaluate success. These sample contests are ranked by ease of use, with one star * indicating a fairly easy contest to put together and three stars *** indicating a more involved contest. Use them as guides as you start to put together your own exciting library contest.

*EARTH DAY COLORING CONTEST

Contest planner:
Children's Librarian

How the choice was made: The library's children's department wanted an activity to tie in with Earth Day. The staff decided a contest might be a fun new idea, so it made sense that the children's librarian would plan the event.

Goals:

- Encourage children to read books and magazines about the environment
- Raise awareness about recycling and conservation of resources
- Increase attendance at Earth Day activities in the library

How the goals were determined: One of the children's department's annual goals was to create a book display highlighting a special day or holiday each month. They chose Earth Day in April because it was a little different from the usual Easter tie-ins. They also wanted to be a part of their town's new recycling program by encouraging children to think twice about what they throw away.

Contest type, audience, and theme:
Coloring contest with an Earth Day/Recycling theme targeted to children ages five through nine.

How the type, theme, and audience were determined: The contest planner and the departmental staff wanted their first contest to be fun yet easy to do, so a coloring contest seemed best because it was easy to organize and easy to judge. They also wanted to attract a large number of entries. They decided to give their contest an Earth Day theme to connect to their Earth Day book display. The target audience age was based more on the age appropriateness of the books in their display than on the coloring part of the contest. Their experience with children was that coloring was something that appealed to virtually every age group and was something almost all children could do.

Eligibility criteria:
Entrants must be between the ages of five and nine years old and must reside in the county served by the library. They do not need a library card to enter.

How the eligibility criteria were determined: Staff determined coloring pages would appeal most to children in this age range. Also, they determined children in these ages would likely be discussing Earth Day in school and so would have some familiarity with the subject and therefore be drawn to the contest.

Contest rules:

- Children entering the contest must be between the ages of five and nine years old (the contest planner determined they would not require a verification of age for entry because it would create extra work for the staff without really adding much to the contest).

NOW, PUT THE PLAN IN MOTION: FOUR MODEL CONTESTS

- Contest entries must be made on official forms, using official coloring sheets.
- Forms and coloring sheets may be picked up in the children's department of the library or downloaded from the library's Web site.
- One entry per child.
- Coloring sheets may be filled in and decorated using any type of coloring device, including crayons, markers, colored pencils, paints, pastels, or chalk.
- No embellishments allowed. This includes glitter glue, feathers, stickers, stamps, photographs, writing, and fabric.
- Entrants must be residents of the county served by the library.
- Entries may be mailed in or delivered in person to the children's department. All entries must be received in the library by 9 P.M. on April 15. No entries will be accepted after that time. Do not leave entries in the book drop. Do not submit entries to the circulation desk. If mailing entries, mail enough in advance to allow for delivery by April 15. April 15 is NOT the postmark deadline.
- Entries without proper identification of entrant will not be considered for judging.
- Entries can be picked up at the library after April 30. No entries will be returned by mail.

How the rules were determined: The contest planner sat down with the staff over lunch one day and brainstormed a list of everything they did not want to see or receive with the entries. This list led to rules like "no embellishments" and "one entry per child" as well as the deadlines for receipt of entries. They also discussed the types of children and families who already participated in a lot of library activities as well as the children they would like to encourage to become more active. This led to the idea of putting the entry forms and coloring sheets on the library Web site possibly to attract interest from parents who typically did not bring their children to the library. Being able to see their children's art work on display or coming to an awards presentation might be enough incentive for them to visit the library. Since the circulation staff had one member out on leave, it was decided to have the entries turned in only to the children's department.

Scheduling:
- Time frame—March 25–April 30
- Publicity begins—March 25

- Contest start—March 25, since entry forms and coloring sheets would be available from then on
- Entry deadline—April 15
- Display of entries—April 18–30
- Announcement of winners—April 22 (Earth Day)
- Publicity of winners and display—news coverage of April 22 event, posting of winning entries on library Web site April 22–30
- Prize pick-up—April 22–30

How the schedule was determined: The library's monthly calendar comes out on or about the 25th of each month, so it made sense to start the publicity then because that would be the primary means of promotion. The staff decided three weeks was long enough for children to get their entries in because contest entry was not very complicated. As entries came in, they were put on display throughout the children's department. The staff chose Earth Day as their official winner announcement because they had already planned a big program for that day. This enabled the contest to do double duty, not only being a program in itself but also helping to promote other library programs.

Selection of prize:
The grand prize, drawn from all winning entries, is an Earth Day poster and a recycling bin for cans and bottles to use in the house. Six winners, one per age, will each win a recycling book and coloring pack. All entrants will receive a certificate, bookmark, and Earth Day temporary tattoo. All prizes and entry incentives must be picked up at the library—none will be mailed. Winners will be announced and recognized at the Earth Day program on April 22.

How the prizes were selected: Because one of the contest goals was to encourage children to read about the environment and preservation, books on the subject made a natural choice for prizes. The fact that they were relatively inexpensive was another deciding factor. The library staff was able to get a recycling bin and coloring packs made up of crayons and markers donated from a local discount store. The incentives for all the entrants were available free from the Environmental Protection Agency—http://www.epa .gov/otaq/schoolbus/e_day_resources.htm.

Selecting judges and determining judging criteria:
- Entries will be judged by a panel of three staff members.
- Entries will be judged on creativity, use of color, and neatness. Examples of creativity would include an unusual use of coloring media (such as finger-painting mixed with

chalk) or use of a particular technique like crayon resistance, in which portions of the picture are colored with crayons and then the whole sheet is painted, causing the colored portions to show more prominently.

How judges and judging criteria were selected: Because the staff and contest planner wanted to make the contest as easy as possible, it made sense to use staff members as judges, since they were already on site and would have ample time to review the entries which would be displayed in the children's department for the duration of the contest. Because each entry was to be submitted on a preprinted coloring sheet, the criteria were naturally limited. Neatness was an obvious significant factor. Creativity and use of color were chosen to encourage children to think about a set activity in new and different ways, a skill which nicely translates into problem solving related to environmental protection and preservation.

Promoting the contest:
The contest planner decided, for simplicity's sake, to make use of library promotional methods already in place:

- Library monthly calendar
- Departmental displays
- Library Web site

How promotional decisions were made: The contest planner made the choice to use regular library promotional outlets for three primary reasons. First, their cost was already built into the library's marketing budget, so there would be no additional cost. Second, because these promotional tools were already established and in use, there would be little additional staff time needed for promotion (creating a flyer and writing the calendar blurb, quick and easy staff tasks). Finally, because these were promotional methods the public was already used to seeing and checking for upcoming programs, there was an increased chance for people to see the announcements about this particular program.

Evaluation method(s):
End-of-contest meeting

How the choice was made: The choice to use this very simple evaluative method was made because the planner felt an evaluation form would be overkill, since the judges were staff members. The planner made sure to invite all staff judges and the marketing staff who were involved.

Additional resources for planning coloring contests:
Good theme tie-ins for coloring contests:

- Holidays
- Special days, like Earth Day, Grandparents Day, or Election Day
- Monthly observances, including Black History Month, Women's History Month, National Food Safety Education Month, or National Fire Prevention Month
- Local, regional, or state events or observances, such as Kentucky Writers Day

National Health Information Center's National Health Observances Calendar:
http://www.healthfinder.gov/library/nho/nho.asp

American Library Association's Library Promotions Listing:
http://www.ala.org/ala/events/librarypromotion/librarypromotions.htm

***Chase's Calendar of Events*:**
This is published annually by McGraw-Hill. Your reference department will most likely have a copy of this helpful text.

*GUESS THE NUMBER OF BRICKS IN THE NEW LIBRARY CONTEST

Contest planner:
Marketing coordinator (half-time position)

How the choice was made: Planning a program to heighten awareness of the library and its services is the job of the marketing coordinator, so it made sense for this staff member to plan a contest.

Contest partner:
General contractor for the building project

How the choice was made: She seemed a natural choice for a contest partner because of her close work with all aspects of the building project. Since she had already donated $3,000 for the groundbreaking ceremony, the contest planner decided to ask her to be a partner in the contest as well.

Goals:
- Heighten awareness of the new building project
- Increase attendance at the groundbreaking ceremony
- Create a public relations activity that would involve people of all ages

How the goals were determined: The administration wanted to include people of all ages in the groundbreaking ceremony to heighten the idea that the library belongs to all the people in the town. The library director charged the marketing coordinator to develop a plan that would achieve that goal. Building on the proven success of their last year's new logo design contest, another contest was proposed.

Contest type, audience, and theme:
Guessing the number of bricks in the new building as part of the groundbreaking celebration targeted at people of all ages

How the type, theme, and audience were determined: The marketing coordinator, in consultation with the circulation, reference, and children's staff, wanted an idea that would take little staff time but would have high visibility. Based on the little staff time required for the previous year's logo contest, a contest was the first choice of a way to bring more people to the groundbreaking ceremony for the new library building. It was decided to announce the name of the winner during the groundbreaking ceremonies. The decision to target all ages as possible contestants was made to keep in line with one of the main goals of the contest—involving many people from throughout the community in the groundbreaking activities. That goal also helped in the decision to use a guessing contest, since guessing was seen as something everyone could do, from very young children who would say the first number that popped into their heads to the oldest engineer who knew how to calculate the number of bricks used per square foot.

Eligibility criteria:
All ages eligible, but entrants needed to reside in the library's service area

How the eligibility criteria were determined: Since it was a guessing contest, it was determined that all ages could participate.

Contest rules:
- Those entering the contest must live in the library service area.
- Entrants can have no involvement with the building project or with the architectural firm, contractor, or subcontractors.

- Contest entries must be on the official entry form, available at all library locations and on the library Web site.
- One entry per person.
- Entries may be mailed or delivered in person to any circulation desk entry box. Entries must be received before 9 P.M. on October 30.
- The winner will be the person with the exact number of bricks or the number closest to the exact number of bricks used.
- Entries without proper identification of entrant will not be considered for judging.
- The number of bricks must be written numerically and in words to avoid any confusion caused by legibility.
- In the case of a tie or multiple entries with the exact winning number, a drawing from the tied entries will be held on November 15 to determine the winner.

How the rules were determined: The marketing coordinator met with several circulation staff to get their help and advice about the possible rules. One of the circulation supervisors suggested colorful, easy-to-recognize entry boxes be placed on each circulation desk with clear signage. They felt this would avoid confusion about keeping track of the entries and make the collection of the entries less staff time-intensive. Since many thousands of people who do not come into the library buildings use the library Web site, putting the entry form on the Web site was viewed as a way of possibly getting more people to participate and learn about the new building.

Scheduling:
- Time frame—September 15–November 15
- Publicity begins—September 15
- Contest start—September 15–October 30
- Entry deadline—October 30
- Announcement of winners—November 15
- Prize pick-up—November 15 at ceremony
- Publicity of winners—November 15 news coverage and possibly a feature story later

How the schedule was determined: The library needed adequate lead time to let people know about the contest. The staff decided that six weeks would be the right amount of time to build interest in the contest and to let the people schedule to attend the groundbreaking ceremony. Because the staff expected a large number of entries and they knew they would be busy with all the other details about the groundbreaking ceremony, they allowed fifteen days between the close of the contest and the announcement of the winners.

Selection of prize:
There was a single prize for the contest—a $1,000 bill.

How the prize was selected: It was determined that the prize would have to be big enough to entice people both to enter the contest and attend the groundbreaking ceremony. Since the general contractor for the building project had donated $3,000 for the overall festivities, it was decided that $1,000 could go to the contest, leaving enough money for refreshments, chair rental, and other expenses.

Selecting judges and determining judging criteria:
- Two staff members were selected to independently review entries and determine the winning entry. If no one
  had the exact number, they were charged with finding the
  one with the closest number.
- Entries had to be clear and legible, with no question from
  either judge about the number submitted on the form.

How judges and judging criteria were selected: Staff members were selected because they would be the ones collecting the entry boxes and it would make it easy to go through the entries. Multiple entries were discarded. The judging criteria were simple: looking for the correct number legibly written.

Promoting the contest:
The marketing coordinator decided to use both existing library marketing tools and some specifically geared for this contest: the library monthly calendar of events, displays at all circulation desks (including a color picture of the new library and an actual brick from the project), and the library Web site. A painted sign was placed at the building site, advertising the contest and the groundbreaking ceremony. The architect and contractor had an announcement on their Web sites with a link to the library's site for more information and the entry form. Finally, the children's library staff created Bob the Builder displays announcing the contest.

How promotional decisions were made: It was cost effective to use the regular library promotion channels. There was no library cost for the architect and contractor's advertising linkage to the library's Web site or for other direct marketing they did, such as the large sign at the building site. The children's librarians came up with the idea to use Bob the Builder books to promote both the contest and the library's collections becasue Bob the Builder is such a popular icon.

Evaluation method(s):
Interview and evaluation forms

How the choice was made: Because the audience for the contest was a general one and the goals related specifically to public relations and community awareness, the contest planner decided to conduct a quick interview of every tenth person coming into the library for a period of three hours the week before the groundbreaking and the week after the groundbreaking and compare results. The planner also used a pop-up window evaluation form on the contractor's Web site to assess the number of people who participated and what their experience was with the contest.

Additional resources for planning guessing contests:
- *American Libraries* and *American Libraries Direct*; *Library Journal* and *LJ Hotline*; and *School Library Journal* often feature unique guessing contests.
- Local newspapers and magazines may have feature stories on unique contests or activities in the community that could make a good guessing contest tie-in.
- *Guinness Book of World Records* may help stimulate creative ideas for guessing contests.

**CREATE A CLOTHING ACCESSORY FROM DUCT TAPE CONTEST

Contest planner:
Librarian assistant and the children's librarian

How the choice was made: Staff had been discussing the idea in the break room over lunch one day, and two staff members in particular were very excited about the possibilities a duct tape contest presented. The librarian assistant had actually entered such a contest when he was in college, so he knew it was something that would appeal to a wide range of ages. The children's librarian had put together a duct tape display the previous fall and had wanted to do a contest for children at that point but was unable to work it out.

Goals:
- Bring more people into the library
- Create an event that ties the local library to a larger national trend

- Stage a fun event for people of all ages to test their ingenuity

How the goals were determined: The library staff wanted to increase the traffic flow in the library during the summer vacation months when they typically saw a drop in visits by their "regulars." They also wanted a way to connect what they were doing on a local level to a popular national event or series of events. Since duct tape contests were springing up all over the country, it seemed to be an ideal way to capture the national buzz.

Contest type, audience, and theme:
Creative construction or fabrication contest with an emphasis on ingenuity with limited resources. Targeted to all ages.

How the type, theme, and audience were determined: Because it was summer, the staff determined they wanted to do a fun contest that would allow people to work on making something, potentially taking advantage of doing something outside and working together as a family. They also thought that people would have more time actually to make something during the slower summer months and that parents might be looking for something for their children to do as well. They decided to include all ages for this same reason.

Eligibility criteria:
Anyone residing in the library service area could participate

How the eligibility criteria were determined: Since one of the main contest goals was to attract more traffic into the library, staff and planners felt opening it up to everyone would better help achieve that goal.

Contest rules:
- Entrants are allowed to use only one roll of duct tape per entry
- One entry allowed per contestant
- Contestants must use the duct tape provided by the library
- No additional materials may be used
- Entries must clearly fit within the contest's topic, Clothing Accessories
- Duct tape may not be affixed to existing accessories
- Entries must be received in the library by 5 P.M. on the deadline day
- Entrants must pick up their entries by 5 P.M. on July 25— unclaimed entries will be disposed of

- Entries without proper identification will not be considered for judging

How the rules were determined: Contest planners wanted to test participants' ingenuity in creating something usable with a limited amount of materials, hence the one-roll-per-entry requirement. To ensure evenness in the entries, everyone had to use exactly the same kind of tape. While many national contests invite participants to embellish an existing item with duct tape, planners for this contest wanted the contest to focus solely on the tape and what people could do with it.

Scheduling:
- Time frame—June 25–July 25
- Publicity begins—June 1
- Contest start—June 25 to pick up materials and specific instructions
- Entry deadline—July 10
- Display of entries—July 11–25
- Announcement of winners—July 21
- Publicity about and display of winners—July 21–25
- Prize pick-up—July 21–25

How the schedule was determined: Contest planners decided to hold the contest for one month only, right in the middle of summer. The short time span fell within their annual Summer Reading program, so they knew they would draw some entries from the increased traffic from that program. General publicity began June 1, but specific details were not made available until the day the contest started so that everyone would have the same time period for creating their entries.

Selection of prize:
- Two grand prizes: $20 gift certificates to a local home improvement store, framed certificates
- Four honorable mentions: A roll of duct tape and a framed certificate
- Prizes had to be picked up in person

How the prizes were selected: One of the contest planners approached the home improvement store about donating rolls of duct tape for contestants. The store manager said that if they could be listed as the sponsor of the contest, they would donate both the tape and gift certificates for prizes.

Selecting judges and determining judging criteria:
- Judging would be by age category: thirteen and under, and fourteen and older
- Half of each entry's score would be determined by a panel of three judges made up of two library staff and the sponsoring store manager
- The other half of each score would be determined by popular vote
- Entries would be judged on creative use of tape, realistic likeness to the clothing accessory, and actual usability of the item

How the judges and judging criteria were selected: The planning staff felt that dividing entries into two age groups would make the competition fairer. They also wanted those visiting the library to be able to vote on the entries, but the logistics of that were a bit challenging because they wanted to avoid situations in which one person could vote five times for one entry, for example. They circumvented this challenge by having signs clearly stating that only one vote per person was allowed and by having a person fill out a ballot for his or her vote. Multiple entries were discarded. The criteria were determined largely by the nature of the entries, combining utility and realism with creativity.

Promoting the contest:
- Teaser announcement in library calendar
- Colorful posters displayed at the library and the sponsoring home improvement store, including a display in the duct tape section of the store
- Section on the library's Web site announcing the contest and providing links to helpful duct tape hints and history

How promotional decisions were made: The staff and planners wanted the contest to be a fun, non-labor-intensive event, so they chose a simple promotional route. The posters were easy to produce and display. They generally announced the contest in the library's calendar, but only so far as to give the contest dates and the general guidelines. They did not announce the specific topic, Clothing Accessories, until the official contest launch to avoid anyone having an unfair time advantage.

Evaluation method(s):
Evaluation form of 4–5 questions; check of door count before, during, and after the contest

How the choice was made: Because one of the contest goals was to have fun, the quick rating evaluation form seemed to be an easy method of assessing the participants' experience with the contest. Questions asked such things as how much participants enjoyed the contest and how likely they were to enter future contests.

Additional resources for planning duct tape contests:
- The Duck Tape Club™, official site of Henkel Duck Tape®:

  www.ducktapeclub.com—This site features many activities using tape, as well as other contests.
- The Duct Tape Guys:

  www.ducttapeguys.com—This humorous site offers realistic ideas, duct tape products like bumper stickers and mugs for sale, and funny duct tape images and scenarios.

***ONE BOOK, ONE CITY ESSAY CONTEST

Contest planner:
Library's program coordinator

How the choice was made: Planning and organizing events tied to the annual One Book event were part of the program coordinator's job description. Decisions for the contest and the overall One Book activities were made by the library's program committee consisting of youth services librarians, adult services librarians, marketing staff, and outreach services staff.

Contest partner(s):
Library foundation, high school teachers, and librarians

How the choice was made: The library foundation director was looking for ways to get involved with specific library projects, and the essay contest provided a high-profile opportunity. High school teachers and librarians were logical partners because the target audience was high school students and the book was on the required reading list.

Goals:
- Plan One Book activities that would draw participation from local high schools
- Create an activity that would encourage students to read the selected book

Lexington Public Library Foundation presents:

One Book One Lexington Essay Contest

One winner - $500 College Scholarship

- Open to all high school seniors in Lexington schools (must be enrolled as a senior 2005-2006 academic year)
- 1000-1,500 words
- A winner will be announced on Monday, May 1, 2006
- The winning essay will be published on the website: **onebookonelexington.org**
- Entries may be turned in at any Lexington Public Library location, or may be mailed to:

Lexington Public Library
140 East Main Street
Lexington, KY 40507
ATTN: Essay Contest

- Deadline is 5PM Friday, April 21, 2006
- Call 231-5549 if you have questions
- All entries must contain name, school and contact information and should be on a sheet separate from the text of the essay
- Essays should address the following question:

"What makes *The Great Gatsby* a book that the whole community should read?"

Zelda Fitzgerald, *Times Square*, 1944, Courtesy of Samuel J. Lanahan

Zelda By Herself:
The Art of Zelda Fitzgerald

July 1-30
Central Library Gallery

Reception: July 7, 5:30-7 PM

Lexington Public Library
140 East Main St.
Lexington, KY 40507

Figure 10-1. One Book One Lexington Essay Contest
(Reproduced by permission of the Lexington Public Library.)

- Strengthen programming partnerships between the public library and high school libraries

How the goals were determined: The public library programming committee wanted to encourage participation in annual One Book activities by area teens. Early in the planning process, they invited area high school librarians and teachers to a joint planning meeting. The high school librarians in the planning meeting identified concerns about paying for college as one of the top concerns for high school juniors and seniors. Several librarians mentioned other scholarship contests held at the schools that had good participation.

Contest type, audience, and theme:
Essay contest on a theme related specifically to the One Book title; for high school seniors

How the type, theme, and audience were determined: The joint planning process between the high schools and the public library led to the decision to hold an essay contest, based on the high school teachers' and librarians' recommendations. The topic of the essay was one that showed the significance of reading the book as a community activity. Although there was much debate on the target audience and whether or not to involve juniors and seniors, the decision was finally made to limit the entries to seniors because they would have the keenest interest in college scholarship opportunities. Plus, the chosen book was on the junior reading lists for most of the schools, so the planning committee knew seniors would already have some familiarity with the book.

Eligibility criteria:
High school seniors within the public library's service county

How the eligibility criteria were selected: The committee wanted to include all high school seniors in the county served by the public library. This included public and private schools and homeschoolers. The limited eligibility group was determined primarily by the fact that they were the ones likely to have the most interest in the project because of the scholarship attached.

Contest rules:
- Entries may be mailed to the library or dropped off at any library location
- The essay itself serves as the contest entry form
- Essay length is at least 1,000 words but not more than 1,500 words
- Essay must have a cover sheet with the entrant's name, school, and contact information

- All essays must be typed and double-spaced
- Essays must significantly address the proscribed topic
- No late entries will be accepted

How the contest rules were determined: In order to make it easy for the contest entrants to enter, the planning committee decided to allow students to mail or drop off their entries. They decided against a contest entry form. This eliminated the staff time needed to design a form, the cost to print the form, the staff time to distribute the form, and the inconvenience to the student to get the form. Since the planning and organization of the contest involved so many partners, the planning committee decided to have all questions directed to one central library phone number.

Scheduling:
- Contest time frame—March 11–April 21
- Publicity begins—March 11 with the public announcement of the One Book, One City selected title for that year
- Contest start—March 11
- Entry deadline—April 12
- Announcement of winner—April 21 at the One Book closing gala event

How the schedule was determined: While planning for the overall One Book events began ten months before the celebratory month, the actual contest length was fairly short because it needed to be completed within the One Book event timeline. The contest came after spring break but long enough before the end of the school year that possible entrants were not struggling with "senioritis."

Selection of prize:
$500 scholarship

How the prize was selected: The committee decided on the relatively small amount of $500 because they thought it would be fairly easy to get. The $500 fit into the range of other small scholarship competitions being held at the schools. The high school librarians had reinforced that $500 was a high enough amount to draw significant interest. Also, it was thought that if the essay contest was highly successful, it would be easier to ask for a bigger amount in subsequent years. The public library foundation director and board chair were approached by the program coordinator to solicit sponsorship of the prize. They gave the initial go-ahead, and the foundation board approved funding the contest. The first hurdle had been successfully jumped. It was agreed that the foundation would receive sponsorship publicity for the essay contest.

Selecting judges and determining judging criteria:
Panel of three judges, assessing the entries on length, writing skills, creativity, grammar, style, originality, and pertinence of the essay to the topic

How judges and criteria were selected: The judging period was only nine days, so it was imperative to select judges who agreed to be available for reading during this short time, who were knowledgeable about the book and what constitutes good writing, and who were flexible because it was not possible to determine ahead of time how many entries would actually be received. Three judges were chosen: the library director, an English faculty member, and a scholar from a local university whose area of expertise was the author of the selected One Book title. By following a wide range of eligibility criteria, the panel of judges was able to use some of the criteria, such as length, as a means of filtering the group of entrants down to a final set.

Essay contests can generate a lot of reading material for judges (see Figure 10-2). Make sure judges have adequate time to read entries and make their selection of the winner or winners.

Promoting the contest:
- Library monthly calendar and Web page
- One Book promotional materials, such as flyers, posters, and bookmarks

Figure 10-2. Essay Contests Can Generate a Lot of Reading Material

- Distribution of flyers in area high schools and at information fairs held throughout the contest period

How promotional decisions were made: The promotion of the contest was fairly easy and straightforward because it was a part of a much larger promotional campaign for the entire One Book program. The main goal of the promotion was to get the pertinent information out to high school seniors in enough time for them to write an essay and submit it.

Evaluation method(s):
End-of-contest meeting

How the choice was made: Because the contest partners were involved early on in the project through a series of meetings, an end-of-contest meeting was a logical concluding event.

CONCLUSION

After the last entry has been tallied and filed away, after the photographs have been taken and returned to their owners, after the last piggy bank has been returned and the last poster taken down, you might be thinking, "Where do I go from here?" The end of a contest is really just the beginning. Do you want to do it again? Consult with your partners, participants, and fellow staff members to determine if a contest should become an annual event. Was it worth the effort? That is something you and your team must determine for yourselves. If your contest increased door traffic, built successful partnerships, or strengthened community interest and involvement, you have created something worthwhile. Keep in mind that it does not matter so much where you end up; it is the getting there that makes it fun.

BIBLIOGRAPHY AND RESOURCES

The American Heritage Dictionary of the English Language, 4th Edition. 2000.

American Library Association. *A Communications Handbook for Libraries*. 2004.

Bergstrom, Joan M., and Craig Bergstrom. *All the Best Contests for Kids: 1990–1991*. Berkley, CA: Ten Speed Press, 1990.

Cavitt, Deborah. "38 Steps to a Well-Rounded PR Program," *Library Talk* 11, no. 1 (January–February 1998).

Fischer, Audrey. "A National Celebration: Library's Bicentennial Reaches Across the Nation," *The Library of Congress Information Bulletin* (August–September 2000), http://www.loc.gov/loc/lcib/00089/celebration.html (accessed 5/30/2006).

Florida, Richard. *The Rise of the Creative Class: And How It's Transforming Work, Leisure, Community and Everyday Life*. New York: Basic Books, 2002.

Fortune, Beverly. "Not All Trophies Are Prized: Kids Love Them; Adults Prefer Cash," *Lexington (KY) Herald-Leader* (February 5, 2005): E-1.

Internet School Library Media Center. "School Library Media Day," http://falcon.jmu.edu/~ramseyil/libslmday.htm (accessed 5/30/2006).

Karp, Rashelle S., ed. *Powerful Public Relations: A How-to Guide for Libraries*. Chicago: American Library Association, 2002.

Lears, T. J. Jackson. *Something for Nothing: Luck in* America. New York: Viking, 2003.

Lundin, Stephen C., Harry Paul, and John Christensen. *Fish! A Remarkable Way to Boost Morale and Improve Results*. New York: Hyperion, 2000.

Merriam-Webster's Collegiate Dictionary 10th Edition. Springfield, MA: Merriam-Webster, Inc., 1993.

Missoula Public Library Internet Branch. http://www.missoula.lib.mt.us/signup.html.

Pfannenstiel, Brenda. "Practically Speaking: Programs on a Low Budget," *School Library Journal* 28, no. 6 (February 1982): 43.

Sachs, Elizabeth. "There's a Pig in the Library!" *School Library Journal* 42, no. 4 (April 1996): 44.

Scotton, Donald W. *Merchant Sponsored Incentive Contests for Retail Employees.* University of Illinois Bureau of Business Management. Bulletin No. 817. Vol. 58, no. 77 (May 1961).

" 'Seussamania' in Geisel's Hometown," *American Libraries* 17, no. 6 (June 1986): 485.

Stewart, Joan. *Clever Contests That Will Tempt Reporters to Call.* Racine, WI: www.101PublicRelations.com, 2003.

University of Minnesota Libraries. http://www.lib.umn.edu/.

Walters, Suzanne. *Library Marketing That Works!* New York: Neal-Schuman Publishers, Inc., 2004.

Washington Library Media Association Website. http://www.wlma.org/Association/sasquatch.htm.

Wolfe, Lisa A. *Library Public Relations, Promotions, and Communications: A How-to-Do-It Manual,* 2nd Edition. New York: Neal-Schuman Publishers, Inc., 2005.

Woodward, Janet. "She's Got a Winner," *School Library Journal* 47, no. 4 (April 2001): 43.

INDEX

ABOUT THE AUTHORS

Kathleen R. T. Imhoff is the Executive Director/CEO of the Lexington Public Library in Lexington, Kentucky. An M.L.S. graduate of the University of Wisconsin-Madison, she is a well-known lecturer, writer, workshop leader, technology innovator, and change agent.

Having worked as a director in small, rural libraries, a medium-sized library, a state library agency and major urban libraries, she brings a unique perspective to marketing and promotion of libraries and their services in all types of libraries. As Assistant Director of the Broward County Library in Ft. Lauderdale, Florida, she supervised the Marketing Department. The Broward County Library won a John Cotton Dana Award for its Better Libraries for a Better Library Bond Campaign. During her tenure in Broward, the library was named LJ/Gale 1996–97 Library of the Year. She has taught Marketing classes for both Syracuse University and the University of South Florida.

An active member of state, regional, national, and international library associations, she has served two terms as Councilor of the American Library Association, was a member of the John Cotton Dana Committee, President of the Public Relations Section and twice President of the Public Library System Section of the Public Library Association.

Kathleen was the recipient of the ALA/PLA/CLSI International Study Award, recipient of the Bumblebee Cannot Fly Award, recipient of the SEFLIN (Southeast Florida Library Information Network) Distinguished Service Award and is a dedicated advocate for improving library services to all.

Ruthie Maslin is a writer and educator and is Outreach Services Manager for the Lexington Public Library in Kentucky. Fairly new to the library world, she spent the first part of her career as a newspaper and broadcast journalist, later becoming involved in literary arts and adult literacy/ English as a Second Language programming in the non-profit sector. The move to public librarianship seemed a natural one, and she is currently near completion of her MSLS degree from the University of Kentucky.

She also teaches developmental reading and writing at the local community college. Author of the *Insider's Guide to Lexington & Kentucky Bluegrass* (1994), she has written extensively for local, regional, and national print and Web-based publications, and she is the recipient of several Kentucky Press Association awards.